VISITING
CHINA'S
PAST

VISITING CHINA'S PAST

A Guide to Sites and Resources

Robert L. Thorp

FLOATING WORLD EDITIONS

First edition, 2006

Published by Floating World Editions, Inc., 26 Jack Corner
Road, Warren, CT 06777. Protected by copyright under the
terms of the International Copyright Union; all rights reserved.
Except for fair use in book reviews, no part of this book may be
reproduced for any reason by any means, including any method
of photographic reproduction, without the permission of the
publisher. Printed in the U.S.A.

ISBN 1-891640-33-X

Library of Congress Cataloging-in-Publication data:

Contents

Preface

I have written this guide for anyone interested in the history and archaeology of China, but especially for those hoping or planning to travel there.

For the amateur archaeologist or dedicated history enthusiast, *Visiting China's Past* offers a rapid introduction to archaeology in China, its links to history, and an overview of major sites and finds. Much of what I discuss here about specific discoveries is also applicable to a whole class of sites. All of the topics are important in any assessment of China's diverse and long-lasting civilization.

For the traveler in China, the guide presents entries introducing twenty-four important sites, all of which can (and should) be visited. The essays situate individual finds in their larger historical and archaeological settings, make references to similar or related finds elsewhere, and suggest further reading.

How to Use this Guide

Entries are arranged by historical chronology; periods are introduced briefly at the beginning of each part. Sites are positioned on a Chronology of Sites (p. 28) and displayed on a Map of Sites (p. 30) for quick reference. Complete publication information for the Suggested Readings given at the end of each chapter is listed in a Bibliography (p. 284).

How to Prepare for an Archaeological Trip to China

You will gain more from any trip to China (or from reading this guide), if you have basic familiarity with Chinese geography, history, and archaeology. While many recent maps and travel guides are available, there is still no really satisfactory introduction to Chinese cultural geography in English. Possible readings include: Yi-fu Tuan, *China* (1969), Caroline Blunden and Mark Elvin, *A Cultural Atlas of China* (1983), and (for contemporary topics) Robert Benewick and Stephanie Donald, *The State of China Atlas* (2005). For Chinese history, Patricia Buckley Ebrey's *The Cambridge Illustrated History of China* (1996) is recommended. For art and archaeology, see Robert L. Thorp and Richard Ellis Vinograd, *Chinese Art and Culture* (2001).

Websites can also be useful; see the Institute of Archaeology (Beijing) at www.archaeology.net.cn (click on "English") and the *China Heritage Newsletter*, published quarterly by Australia National University online at www.chinaheritagenewsletter.org.

Acknowledgments

Many thanks to five people who made this book possible: Linda Feinstone, Ray Furse, Freda and Chris Murck, and not least Karen Brock.

Reinventing the Past: Archaeology in China

Although early travelers from abroad sometimes encountered China's past in the form of ruins like the Great Wall, today's visitor is privileged to experience sights that have been unknown, even beyond imagination, for many centuries. Today, a trip through China is a journey through time, from the pit dwellings of a Neolithic farming community to the splendors of a Ming imperial tomb, from the creations of an anonymous lapidary working jade to the indelible personality of a larger-than-life historical figure like the First Emperor of Qin. Indeed, we know more about the past, especially its early episodes, than anyone has been able to know since ancient times. The agent making all of this possible is archaeology.

It was not always so. In pre-modern times, scholars in China knew the past through texts, the words of their predecessors as written down in chronicles and classics, and in dynastic and local histories. In the Western Han period (206 BCE–9 CE), the court historian ("grand scribe" by title) Sima Qian, worked with his father to compile a synthetic text drawn from the literary and historical sources then available. Their creation, best known as the *Records of the Grand Historian (Shi ji),* chronicles the history of the world from the culture heroes of remote antiquity through the "Three Dynasties" (Xia, Shang, and Zhou) down to the recent past, the kingdom and empire of Qin and the successor Han regime, their own. Divided into annals, year-by-year registers of major events at the court,

Imagining the Past

Probing with the Luoyang spade

chronological tables, treatises on major topics of interest to administrators, and biographies of notables, this work became the model for the dynastic histories, from Han through Qing, that followed. The standard histories, most compiled by court officials, have shaped the consciousness of educated men and women in China ever since, and remain no less influential today in determining the agendas of archaeologists. Archaeology is conceived as a discipline within history; the goals of archaeologists are to create new evidence for the writing of history; and the results of archaeology are most often catalogued and exhibited as a material commentary on the historical record.

A tradition of history writing cannot be taken for granted. It is not characteristic of all ancient cultures or their descendants. In China, language and script evolved continuously from very early times without interruption to the present. Scholars of recent times were not cut off from their past by a lost language, as happened in the Indian subcontinent or the Nile Valley. This thread linking past and present has been a precondition for the rise and success of archaeology in China. Countless times, scholars have tested the veracity of the historical record and found material traces that confirmed their suppositions. The names of Shang kings in Sima Qian's "Annals" were found on the bones and shells from Anyang (see below); the traditional date and circumstances of the Zhou conquest were reiterated in a bronze inscription recovered as recently as 1976. Recently, references to the Duke of Zhou—the most esteemed paragon of Confucian virtue in all of early history—have been found on excavated material (Ch. 6, Zhou Yuan). Such confirmations have led Chinese scholars to embrace many parts of their tradition that have not as yet been substantiated by "hard" evidence. The debate over the historicity of the Xia, now commonly identified with the Erlitou Culture of Henan, is a case in point. Many scholars outside China remain dubious of this claim, and their reservations highlight another component of traditional historiography: myth.

From the oldest written sources—oracle-bone and bronze inscriptions—it would seem that the ancient peoples of North China lacked an evolved set of mythic traditions: accounts of the creation of the world or the invention of the elements of civilized society. Such accounts are barely hinted at in the oldest transmitted texts, like parts of the *Book of Songs (Shi jing),* and appear in more developed forms only in the latter part of the Zhou, the centuries leading up to Qin unification in 221 BCE. Thus records of the Yellow Emperor (Huang Di) or the "Divine Farmer" (Shen Nong), and indeed of the Xia, are far removed in time from those eras. Moreover, these accounts have many of the hallmarks of writers synthesizing disparate traditions to create a body of mytho-history. Miraculous births and heroic deeds strain modern credulity. Today, when such mytho-history is adduced to identify material evidence, such as the tomb of the Yellow Emperor in Shaanxi or sites of the Erlitou Culture as Xia, cautious scholars raise a red flag. Of course, it is not impossible that a people who called themselves Xia will one day be confirmed, perhaps by actual inscriptions from a proper dig. (In fact we have a mix of both hard evidence and myth for the Shang and Zhou.) But for now, hard evidence for both the culture heroes and the Xia kings known to Sima Qian is lacking.

"Doubting Antiquity" became a fashion in the early twentieth century among critical historians who had observed the inverse relationship between accounts of early figures and the actual dates of the texts that supplied information about them. The later the texts, the more complete the data, a suspicious coincidence. Even as we admire their acumen, we must recognize that archaeology is far more than a

Oracle-bone

Oracle-bone inscription rubbing

handmaiden to history. Excavations and interpretation create new knowledge, overturning the conventional wisdom of even the most critical of critics. A powerful example is the discovery, at the turn of the twentieth century, of "oracle-bones," the oldest writing in East Asia and the primary sources for our study of the first historic dynasty, the Shang (c. 1600–c. 1050 BCE). These inscriptions, incised on the shells of turtles and the shoulder blades of oxen, usually bear specific day-dates, and are often datable to a king's reign. We often know the name of the diviner cracking bones or shells, and the subject of the divination: weather, childbirth, harvest, or the prospects for an impending battle. Sometimes we learn actual outcomes: whether it rained or a birth was auspicious. With hard work and some educated guess work, these inscriptions offer a history of the world of the Shang kings. While these sources only became known after 1900, leading to the excavations at Anyang which continue today (Ch. 4, Anyang), the names of many of the Late Shang kings were already attested in writings of the following Zhou period (c. 1050–221 BCE) transmitted through the centuries. Thus the discovery of these earliest writings and especially their point of origin complicated the task of "Antiquity Doubters" and more conventional historians alike.

Similarly, in the early twentieth century, a well-informed scholar at the Field Museum in Chicago, Berthold Laufer (1874–1934) could assert that China had never witnessed a New Stone Age, and based on the best evidence then available, he was correct. But since the 1920s, and especially the 1950s, a vast quantity of data for Neolithic cultures in every region of modern-day China has been amassed (Ch. 2, Banpo, and Ch. 3, Liangzhu), prefacing history with evidence for the development of human societies over several millennia. Some of this evidence, in turn, may well be reflected, however indirectly and imperfectly, in the myths rejected by critical scholars.

After the unification of the First Emperor, the historical record is vital to identifying and understanding almost every kind of archaeological find, from the remains of walls and palaces, to burials large and small, to workshops or the foundations of a Buddhist pagoda. Few cultures have the depth and breadth of records that can be brought to bear on the archaeology of China's imperial era. Humble graves of convict laborers who died building the walls of Han Luoyang yield crude brick inscriptions recording their names, native places, and even their sentences. The Han history in turn tells us of the officials under the Court Architect who were charged with the convicts' burials. Also with excavations come important new discoveries of primary sources, from epitaphs in Tang tombs written out by notable scholars of the day to bureaucratic records on bamboo slips, silk, and paper from early dynasties. Archaeology in recent decades has produced significant increases in the primary stuff of history, and hence has facilitated specialized research into such topics as law, land-holding, and taxation. When the house of a famous person, like Bo Juyi the Tang poet, is identified, it resonates for Chinese scholars and the public at large, rather as sites linked to George Washington or Abraham Lincoln might for an American. So while some discoveries are impressive on their face—several thousand terra cotta warriors take anyone's breath away—the appreciation of others requires some grounding in Chinese history or literature. In this sense, history and archaeology remain inseparable. With the exception of three prehistoric sites introduced first in this book, every find is discussed in relation to the historical record.

Investigating the Past

Like other European inventions such as steam locomotives and hospitals, for example, archaeology came to China in the nineteenth century. No word for the then immature discipline existed, so a phrase from literary tradition was co-opted: *kao gu* (examining the past). This newly-minted phrase evoked the long-standing tradition of antiquarian scholarship, by which scholar-amateurs collected ancient things and assayed their historical value. Gathering together ancient bronzes and jades or making rubbings of inscriptions cut into stone were recognized pursuits (known as *jin shi xue*) that could supplement or correct the historical record. A scholar examining an inscribed bronze ritual vessel might learn how a word was written in the Zhou, and perhaps thereby correct a statement in an early lexicon about that word. A rubbing might have a clear date—reign, year, month, and day—that, in turn, would enable the diligent scholar to correct the date for the same event found in a history. The old stone, made at the time in question, was undoubtedly more reliable than the many-times-copied text, many-times-cut printing blocks of a history. This attitude was shared by Chinese scholars and the Western archaeologists who came to China. Thus while archaeology as a fieldwork practice was decidedly foreign and new, its utility fit snugly into the mind-set of the educated Chinese elite. Other aspects of archaeology did give traditional scholars pause. Opening graves was taboo and unfilial, and objects from them were bad luck, of no interest in themselves. Only gradually did such reservations give way to what we now take as common sense.

The first notable excavations in the territory of the People's Republic of China took place in Central Asia. European and Japanese scholars pursued geographical and historical agendas back and forth across the fringes of the Takla Makan desert and Turpan basin in what is now Xinjiang (Ch. 16, Jiaohe, and Ch. 20, Mogao). There were many colorful actors in these adventures, and some of their work holds up today. It is hard for us to imagine a foreign archaeologist making off with the cultural treasures of another people without "permission" from the authorities. Claims that the locals did not appreciate what they had or would have vandalized it are not very credible in most cases, but among Chinese archaeologists today that is water under the bridge. International cooperation rules the day. So at the Mogao cave-chapels, Astana cemetery, or Han "long walls" that Aurel Stein (1862–1943) investigated, his work is a foundation for contemporary scholarship, which matches his results with new finds and expands on the understandings his collaborators first proposed.

Chinese archaeology practiced by Chinese archaeologists had to wait until the 1920s, and this work came on three fronts. At the beginning of the decade, a Swedish geologist, J.G. Andersson (1874-1960), reported evidence for Neolithic "painted pottery" at sites in western Henan and the Gansu corridor. Within a few years, a newly-minted Harvard-trained anthropologist named Li Ji (Li Chi, 1896–1979) had excavated related material in nearby Shanxi. At much the same time Andersson turned his

Excavation of royal tomb
M1004, Anyang

attention to "Dragon Bone Hill" outside Peking, and employed a European scholar, Otto Zdansky, to dig there for fossils. Within a few years a Chinese archaeologist, Pei Wenzhong (1904–1982), recovered a fossil hominid skullcap, now immortalized as "Peking Man" (Ch. 1, Zhoukoudian). And by the end of the decade, the Archaeology Section of the newly-founded Academia Sinica led by Li Ji was prospecting near Anyang for oracle-bones. As a modern scholarly practice, Chinese archaeology grew out of these several projects, all of which gained worldwide attention in the prewar decades.

Pioneers like Pei Wenzhong and Li Ji pursued their new vocation with a blend of Chinese and non-Chinese assumptions and agendas. The oracle-bones made identification of the Anyang sites relatively unproblematic, and the excavators were soon talking of the "ruins of Yin" (a phrase found in a Han commentary to Sima Qian). Thus for the Bronze Age, archaeology required skills at excavation and epigra-

phy, mastery of sorting pottery and surveying foundations as well as the ability to decipher inscriptions and
run down historical sources. Understanding the
painted pottery was more difficult. The known sample
was so small and control of stratigraphy so limited that
only the broadest identifications could be suggested:
perhaps Xia, perhaps earlier. Sorting out the Neolithic
evidence has required decades of additional, widespread excavations that permit a much broader understanding, as well as modern scientific dating
techniques. So too with Peking Man. A truly international and multi-disciplinary investigation from the
outset, the work there only regained this cast in the
1990s when international collaboration resumed. In
all three cases, interpretations have changed steadily as
new data and especially new strategies for making
sense of the evidence have developed. Thus the "Cave
Home of Peking Man" is not quite that any more, but
the site retains its significance as one of the richest
concentrations of evidence for early man anywhere.

Managing the Past

For most observers outside the PRC, Chinese archaeology burst onto the world stage in the 1970s with
"The Chinese Exhibition," first in Europe and Japan,
and then Canada and the U.S. Until King Tut, this
"exhibition of archaeological finds from the People's
Republic" was the most attended in the history of the
museums that hosted it, and media coverage was
extensive. In many ways it fed the frenzy to travel to
China after 1979 when the U.S. and PRC normalized
relations. The beautiful things on display, however,
were the products of policies and practices that had
begun in the 1950s, the continuing productivity of
Chinese archaeology no less so. Without such policies

in place—laws, an administrative structure, a corps of trained archaeologists—the likelihood that much of China's past would have been destroyed during the 1950s to 1980s is very high. Large-scale work on "basic construction" (infrastructure) in the 1950s threatened many sites and monuments, and the phenomenal growth of the economy since the late 1970s would surely have doomed many others.

For the last fifty years, "things from the past with scientific, historical, or artistic value" have been defined, by law, as "cultural relics" (wen wu), and hence entitled to protection by the state. The broad scope of this definition was apparent in "The Chinese Exhibition" where Neolithic bone needles (from Banpo) were juxtaposed with fossilized Tang-era pastries (from Turpan) and blue-and-white porcelain from the ruins of Khubilai Khan's capital (Beijing). The category of "cultural relics" encompasses most of the material culture and cultural heritage of the area we now call China prior to recent times (sites associated with the Communist Revolution are included). Historic buildings, Buddhist temples and cave-chapels, stone monuments, every species of art and craft, archaeological sites and artifacts, all warrant the ministrations of local, provincial, and national governments. Unlike the U.S., everything underground belongs to the state. And as in most of the world, Chinese archaeologists work for the state, through universities and institutes at both the national and provincial levels.

In principle, locations to be developed for new construction must be surveyed by archaeologists prior to that work. If archaeological remains are identified, "salvage" excavation goes forward prior to construction, and sometimes the project must be changed to preserve a site. Indeed, a very high percentage of the discoveries, large and small, treated in this volume, have been uncovered through salvage work. (See for example the Han imperial tomb, Ch. 10, Yangling.) Several nationwide surveys have been conducted in China. Five lists promulgated by the State Council between 1961 and 2003 now protect 1268 national sites, along with 101 "historic cities" and thirty-one World Heritage designations. Thousands more are enrolled on provincial and local lists. Many sites are being developed through further investigations, with the result that archaeology actually takes a formative role in creating new cultural relics, both large and small. Any serious trip to China will involve visits to protected sites, many the direct result of archaeological projects. This guide introduces some two dozen locales, from excavations of a single tomb or pagoda to vast areas that once were thriving dynastic capitals.

Since the 1950s, thousands of archaeologists have been trained. In China today archaeology is taught at over a dozen major universities, which in turn send their graduates to positions in provincial and national institutes. As a discipline, it sometimes exists within a department of history and sometimes stands alone, as at Peking University. The premier professional organization under the wings of the Chinese Academy of Social Sciences is the Institute of Archaeology in Beijing. Founded in 1950, it has a staff of several hundred archaeologists, many now with advanced degrees, as well as other specialists. It is charged with supervising excavations nationwide and itself sends teams into every part of China. Several of China's "ancient capitals," including Erlitou, Anyang (Ch. 4), Luoyang (Ch. 13), and Han-Tang Chang'an (Xi'an, Ch. 17), are under the control of the Institute. The leading journals of archaeology are published by the Institute, as well as a monograph series. Also in Beijing, the Cultural Heritage Administration (formerly known as the Cultural Relics Bureau) not only administers and budgets excavations and museums, but also has it own publishing house, Cultural Relics Press. Another division sends exhibitions abroad.

From the perspective of the Chinese government, archaeology plays several vital roles. It protects and explores the past, both of which have the virtues of instilling pride and creating resources for China and attracting foreign visitors. Archaeology is never far removed from the political and cultural agendas of the day, as true outside of China as within, but no one can deny that the collective achievements of excavators since the 1950s have both remade the history of China and greatly enriched the world's cultural heritage. This guide makes such achievements accessible both for the armchair traveler or student and the visitor on the spot.

Cultural Relics and the National Register

The People's Republic began to exercise control over its cultural heritage through temporary regulations issued in the early 1950s. Extensive surveys have now been conducted several times, most notably in the 1980s, and the number of sites identified has grown to more than 300,000. From the outset, the register of protected sites has recognized a variety of categories in line with the expansive definition of "cultural relics" mentioned. At present, the Cultural Heritage Administration has designated thirty-one UNESCO World Heritage sites, 101 "famous historic cultural cities" (*lishi wenhua ming cheng*), 151 "national important scenic heritage districts" (*guojia zhongdian fengjing*

National Register marker at Ta'er Si

mingsheng chu), and 1268 "protected national important cultural relics sites" (*quanguo zhongdian wenwu baohu danwei*). The World Heritage Sites are of three types: natural, cultural, and "cultural-scenic." This guide introduces five UNESCO sites: Zhoukoudian (Ch. 1), Anyang (Ch. 4), Lishan (Ch. 9), Mogao (Ch. 20), and the Ming Valley (Ch. 24). The list of protected historic cities includes all the imperial capitals; here we include six of the "seven great ancient capitals:" Anyang, Xi'an (Ch. 17), Luoyang (Ch. 13), Hangzhou (Ch. 22), Nanjing (Ch. 14), and Beijing (Ch. 23), as well as Jiangling, the area of the ancient Chu capital (Ch. 8).

Since 1961, the national register has been expanded five times. Starting with 180 sites in that year, new groups were announced in 1982 (62), 1988 (258), 1996 (250), and 2001 (518). When each site is enrolled, it has already been studied and an inventory of its historic and cultural assets compiled. Any site listed is afforded both recognition and protection, and as a practical matter allotted some budget and staff. Although this status does not automatically ensure long-term safety, it does make that outcome much more likely. No construction project on or near the site can be undertaken without first consulting with the appropriate authorities. Moreover, protected sites generally become centers for local tourism; they play a positive role in the local economy.

The following five formal categories comprise the national register and listings maintained by cities, counties, and provinces:

Ancient Sites (*gu yizhi*) Total: 285

In this context, "ancient" refers to anything prior to the last dynasty, the Qing (1644–1911). A site can be as modest as a small area without surface features identified simply by a plain concrete roadside marker. All ancient sites, however, have undergone at least partial excavation, and are published in preliminary reports. Some have been the subject of proper monographs, and a few, like Banpo (Ch. 2) and Liangzhu (Ch. 3), support site museums that preserve features of the excavations as well as display artifacts. Ranging from Paleolithic rock shelters and Neolithic villages to defunct cities, like Jiaohe (Ch.16) and Chang'an (Ch. 17), many ancient sites develop over time through

Song tombs, Gongyi, Henan

excavations. However, the desire to preserve features within trenches requires excavators leave some areas intact rather than digging to sterile soil. Thus lower levels remain unknown.

This category has seen the greatest growth in recent decades, and encompasses everything from city walls (such as Ming Xi'an) to halls, pagodas, and pavilions (Ch. 21) within temples, residences, and gardens. The largest complexes (like the Forbidden City, Beijing, or the Potala, Lhasa) are simultaneously ensembles of historic architecture and museums displaying their contents. Intense visitation poses serious challenges to preservation. Many ancient structures, especially those in remote settings, still await renovation.

Ancient Architecture (*gu jianzhu*) Total: 574

The oldest extant wooden buildings in China date to the Tang, while the oldest masonry structures are from the Han (gate-towers) and sixth century (pagodas). Architectural sites often have more recent, but still pre-modern, structures in place, so the dates assigned to them can span many centuries. This category ignores function and ethnicity. Thus Buddhist temples, Muslim mosques, and other "minority" buildings are extended recognition.

This category includes many sites introduced here, from Lishan (Ch. 9), and the Han (Ch. 10), Tang (Ch. 18), and Ming (Ch. 24) imperial tombs to such recent excavations as the Nan Yue tomb in Guangzhou (Ch. 11). Thus it blends historic locales long recognized as important burials, and recent finds not known prior to excavation. In scale, tomb sites range from the modest to the immense, such as the Tang necropolises, the Zhaoling and Qianling. A number of underground tomb chambers are open for visitation.

Ancient Tombs (*gu muzang*) Total: 127

Cave-chapels
(*shi ku si*)
Total: 108

Most cave-chapels are Buddhist (Daoist examples also exist) and date to the period of division, Sui, and Tang. Three sites have received the greatest attention—Yungang (near Datong), Longmen (near Luoyang), and Mogao (Dunhuang)—beginning with European and Japanese scholars in the early twentieth century. A number of cave-chapels were "discovered" during field investigations of the 1950s. The practice of archaeology in China continues to incorporate cave-chapels, both through detailed surveys of the chapels and their imagery and through excavations at the foot of the cliffs that reveal early structures or abandoned caves. The majority of cave-chapels are in the North and Northwest, some convenient to ancient capitals, others quite remote. We introduce Mogao, the "Caves of the Thousand Buddhas" at Dunhuang (Ch. 20). This category also incorporates monuments like cliff-face images and inscriptions, and collections of steles and sculpture such as the Beilin in Xi'an.

Revolutionary
Sites and
Architecture
Total: 174

These sites were accorded pride of place heading the first three groups announced in 1961, 1982, and 1988. This has always been a category contingent on the way history is viewed. For example, the Marco Polo Bridge (Lugou Qiao) outside of Beijing, an authentic bridge of the twelfth century, was listed here because it was the site of a skirmish at the beginning of the Anti-Japanese War. Likewise, the Gate of Heavenly Peace, the formal gate to the Ming-Qing Imperial City in Beijing, a fifteenth-century structure, was listed here because on October 1, 1949, the People's Republic was formally proclaimed from its rostrum. Either might equally well have been designated as "ancient architecture."

Beginning in 1996, this category was renamed "modern and contemporary historical sites and representative architecture" to encompass buildings not directly related to the history of the Communist revolution and PRC. This category has become a vehicle for protecting notable buildings of the nineteenth and twentieth centuries, such as those on the Shanghai Bund, as well as domestic architecture. In spite of this preservation strategy, recent architecture has suffered grievously in most Chinese cities as a result of the current economic expansion.

SUGGESTED READING

One of the best introductions to recent Chinese archaeology is *The Golden Age of Chinese Archaeology,* ed. Xiaoneng Yang (1999), which showcases many of the most impressive discoveries since 1949 for the Neolithic, Bronze Age, and early Imperial eras. Yang reviews the development of archaeology, pp. 25–45. This catalogue is complemented by the same editor's two-volume *New Perspectives on China's Past: Chinese Archaeology in the Twentieth Century* (2004). The second volume of this work summarizes 156 major discoveries, including most of those introduced in this guide. Both works are lavishly produced and illustrated, if not portable. A pocket-sized alternative is Corinne Debaine-Francfort, *The Search for Ancient China* (1999), compiled by a practicing archaeologist.

Other exhibition catalogues illustrate and discuss the fruits of archaeology since 1950: *The Chinese Exhibition* (1974); *The Great Bronze Age of China* (1980); *The Quest for Eternity* (1987); *Ancient Sichuan: Treasures from a Lost Civilization* (2001); and *China: Dawn of a Golden Age* (2004), among others.

Chronology of Sites

Prehistory
Lower Palaeolithic
670,000 – 410,000 ya   *H. erectus,* Zhoukoudian (1929★)
Upper Palaeolithic
18,000 ya   *H. sapiens,* Upper Cave (1933-34)
Middle Neolithic
4800-4300 BCE   Banpo village (1953-57)
Late Neolithic
3000-2200 BCE   Liangzhu graves (1986-)

Xia, Shang, and Zhou
1600-1050 BCE   Sanxingdui pits (1986-)
1250-1046 BCE   Anyang (1928-)
1046-771 BCE   Zhou Yuan (1970s-)
7th-3rd c. BCE   Luoyang chariot pits (2002-03)
c. 433 BCE   Suizhou tomb (1978)
5th-3rd c. BCE   Jinan Cheng (1970s/80s-)

Qin and Han
210 BCE   Lishan (1974-)
186-168 BCE   Mawangdui tombs (1971-73)
126 BCE   Yangling, Xi'an (1990-)
122 BCE   Nan Yue tomb (1983)
2nd-1st c. BCE   Jiaohe (Jushi kingdom), Turpan
1st-3rd c. CE   Han-Wei city, Luoyang (Lingtai, Taixue)

Northern and Southern Dynasties
316-589   Jiankang, Nanjing (2001-03) Southern Dynasty tombs
c. 420-40+   Early Mogao chapels, Dunhuang
493/95-534   N. Wei capital, Luoyang
516-534   Yongning Si Pagoda, Luoyang (1963-)
6th-10th c.   Buddhist images, Qingzhou (1996) [Burial 12th c.]

Sui and Tang

582	Chang'an
649	Zhaoling
683	Qianling
783	Nanchan Si, Mt. Wutai
857	Foguang Si, Mt. Wutai
874	Famen Si crypt (1987)

Song, Yuan, and Ming

970s	Leifeng Pagoda, Hangzhou (2001)
984	Guanyin Pavilion, Tianjin
11th c.	Sutra Cave sealed, Dunhuang (1900)
1023–32	Sage Mother Hall, Taiyuan
1056	Wooden Pagoda, Yingxian
1138	S. Song capital, Hangzhou Guan yao kilns (1985/1996)
1267+	Dadu (Cambaluc), Beijing
1424	Changling, Ming valley, Beijing
1620	Dingling, Ming valley (1956–57)

* *Dates in parenthesis indicate discovery or excavation.*

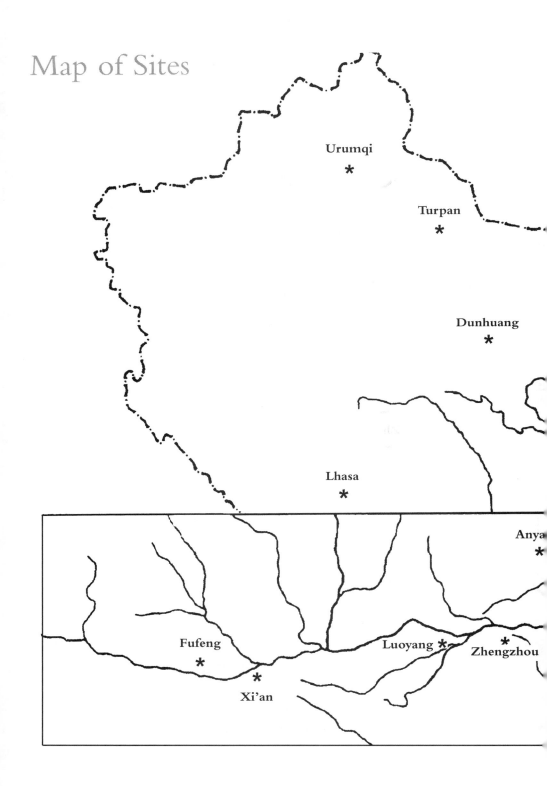

Map of Sites

Urumqi
*

Turpan
*

Dunhuang
*

Lhasa
*

Anya
*

Fufeng
*

Luoyang *

Zhengzhou
*

Xi'an
*

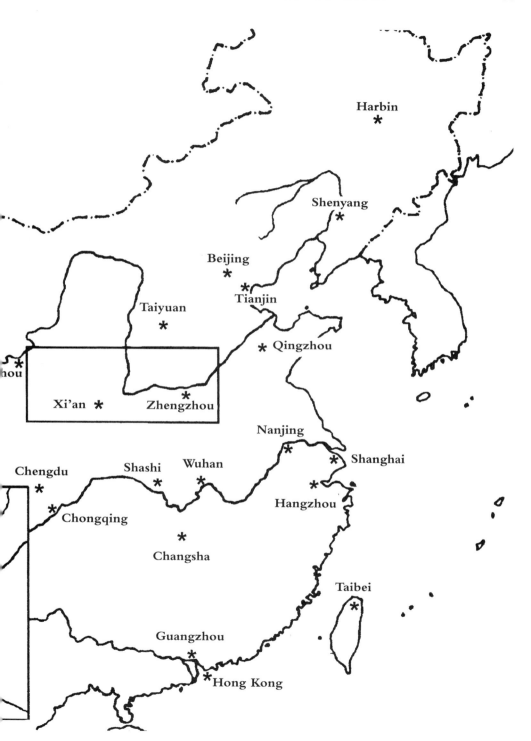

Prehistory

Most of the sites we visit in this book are historical, a term that in China can be defined in several ways. For example, many writers claim that China has a "history of 5000 years," and some authors even begin history with Peking Man (Ch. 1) as much as 700,000 years ago. As used here, however, history begins with the oldest surviving primary sources; by definition, it cannot predate the use of writing. In China Proper writing appears, rather dramatically, at around 1250–1200 BCE. Those writings are the Shang "oracle-bone" inscriptions (*jiagu wen*) and the same graphs employed in bronze inscriptions (*jin wen*). These scripts are the direct ancestors of all later Chinese writing, and in fact are even readable to a limited degree by a literate person today.

Prehistory extends back from the thirteenth century BCE into the eras known by convention as the Neolithic ("new stone") and Paleolithic ("old stone") ages. Using tool-making as a basis to classify ancient cultures originated with the scheme of "Three Ages" (stone, bronze, and iron) invented by a Danish antiquarian in the early nineteenth century. As a standard by which to classify and sequence artifacts, the system has virtues. However, the kinds of tools a culture relies on would seem to have no particular connection to whether or not that culture was also literate. The Maya of Central America and a number of their neighbors had writing, but relied on stone tools, not metals.

In China, Paleolithic is applied to many sites associated with early man. In some cases, stone flakes, tools, and faunal remains may be the only evidence to survive, while at others human fossils accompany such artifacts. Such sites are shared by paleoanthropologists, who focus on the biological evolution of our ancestors, and paleoarchaeologists, who study material culture. In recent decades, several scholars have pointed out that early man in modern-day China, and especially in the south, certainly employed perishable materials like bamboo for a variety of purposes. These materials would not be found with the fossil record. Moreover, most terms for stone tool industries are based on earlier European discoveries; they may be inappropriate for East Asia. Among Chinese scholars, there are several camps on whether or not ancestral human populations reached modern-day China from Africa, and whether or not there was additional evolution within China that would account for "modern humans" there. Some Chinese scholars even regard Paleolithic peoples as the first "Chinese," but this can be true only in a geographical sense. "Chinese culture" only developed long after fully modern humans had populated many parts of the geographical area we label by that word.

By convention the Neolithic has been defined as an age of ground or polished stone tools (axes, adzes, spades) when people lived in settled, village communities, raising domesticated animals and crops, and making pottery (Ch. 2, Banpo). Grinding one stone against another was a later technique than percussion and flaking methods, and hence the distinction between new and old stone ages. Polishing or grinding is also the root of the amazingly sophisticated working of jade and other hard-stones discussed in the entry on Liangzhu (Ch. 3). Viewing prehistoric cultures today, however, one finds many different combinations of traits invoked by the traditional understanding of the Neolithic. For example, settled life and polished stone tools occur without pottery (the aceramic Neolithic of the Fertile Crescent), or elaborate pottery can be found without polished stone tools and within a hunting and gathering life style (the Jomon of Japan).

Today anthropologists prefer to speak in terms of levels of social complexity. The earliest family groups seem to give way over time to small-scale village societies, and sometimes over time to larger units designated as tribes or chiefdoms. Still larger regional polities with population centers and several levels of settlements dispersed across the landscape emerge still later in some areas; these are complex chiefdoms or incipient states. In most discussions, the emergence of the state is the defining trait of "civilization" (in Chinese, *wen ming*), a level of social complexity that did not appear in China Proper until the Bronze Age. While there are clear differences in the societies represented here by Banpo (Shaanxi) and Liangzhu (Zhejiang), there is no consensus yet among scholars as to how precisely to apply Euro-American anthropological models to the current evidence in China.

SUGGESTED   See Chang Kwang-chih and Xu Pingfang, *The*
READING   *Formation of Chinese Civilization: An Archaeological Perspective* (2005) for a recent synthesis by Chinese scholars.

Zhoukoudian: Cave Home of Peking Man

1

PEKING MAN SITE
FANGSHAN, BEIJING
670,000–18,000 YEARS AGO
WORLD HERITAGE SITE

Two major excavations put the archaeology of China on the map in the early twentieth century: Peking Man and Anyang. The discoveries of fossils in the hills southwest of Beijing at Zhoukoudian were an important stepping stone in the international quest to unravel human origins; the site retains its significance in this pursuit today. The excavations near Anyang, Henan (Ch. 4) began the archaeological investigation of the origins of ancient Chinese civilization; this site too has maintained its importance, especially for Chinese scholars and students of comparative civilizations. It is no accident that both sites are inscribed on the UNESCO World Heritage roster, and that both sites remain active today.

In the Chinese scholarly scheme of things, the study of fossil man and his artifacts is assigned to the Institute of Vertebrate Paleontology and Paleoanthropology (IVPP) within the Academy of Sciences. This institute is the lineal descendant of the Cenozoic Research Laboratory established in the 1920s at what was then Peking Union Medical College, funded by Rockefeller foundation grants and sponsored by the Geological Survey of China. The first professionals to work at the Peking Man site were European scholars associated with the Survey, College, and Laboratory, but their Chinese associates quickly assumed the major roles in the work on site. Indeed the first discovery of a human cranium was made by Pei Wenzhong (1904–82) in 1929. During the 1920s to 40s, most of the published analyses of the site, its fossils and artifacts, were produced by an international cohort of scholars, and some of their interpretations clearly derive from their understanding of European prehistory. Since 1949, work has been carried forward by the first generation of Chinese paleoanthropologists and by the several new generations of specialists trained by them. In the last two decades, international collaborators have returned to Zhoukoudian, and debates over these finds have once again become an international conversation.

Main cave (locality no. 1)

Zhoukoudian (spelled "Chou-k'ou-tien" in earlier publications) is a small town 48 km southwest of Beijing nestled against the Western Hills on the edge of the North China Plain. Limestone caves here were known to locals as a rich source of "dragon bones" useful in Chinese medicine, a parallel to the discovery of oracle-bones and Anyang (Ch. 4 below). In 1918, J. G. Andersson (1874–1960), a Swede and a geologist by training, visited the area as a possible source of fossils. (Andersson is equally well-known for his identification of the Yangshao painted pottery Neolithic culture of North China.) By 1921, Andersson had arranged for a young colleague, Otto Zdansky, to excavate in search of ancient horse fossils. The cave that Zdansky began to unearth was on Dragon Bone Hill (Longgu Shan), and had already been exploited by villagers in their hunts for fossils. In two short seasons, 1921 and 1923, Zdansky—unknown to Andersson—found hominid teeth amid his large collection of fossils, which he promptly took back to Sweden. Only in 1926 did word arrive in Beijing of Zdansky's discoveries, and on the basis of the teeth alone, the Canadian anatomist Davidson Black of the Peking Union Medical College coined the term *Sinanthropus Pekinensis,* a daring leap of faith on his part. Dedicated excavations in pursuit of human remains began the following year as a Sino-Swedish collaboration.

Peking Man

Dragon Bone Hill

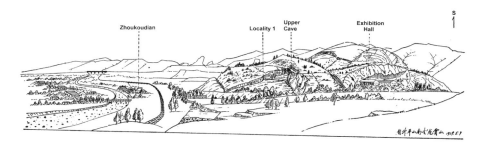

These excavations were centered on a large cave known as locality no. 1. Over time an enormous amount of material (20,000 cubic meters) was removed, much of it breccia, a hardened rocky matrix formed after deposition that had to be broken apart with picks and even explosives. The cave is roughly 140 m east-west by 20 m wide and reaches depths of 50 m. Fossil-bearing deposits were 30 to 40 m thick and are now seen as thirteen distinct levels. As excavators worked the site, they came upon large numbers of animal fossils, 110 species ranging from saber-tooth tigers to hyenas, horses, and deer. They also found traces of fire, some of which were interpreted as hearths, and thousands of stone tools, most (88 percent) quartz flakes from a source about 2 km distant. Most important, the excavators found evidence for about forty individual hominids, including five skull caps and 140 teeth. This quantity of human fossils makes Zhoukoudian the most productive *homo erectus* site in the world, even today. Other localities bearing fossils on the hill were also explored; today more than forty-five are known. Some of these deposits are much older than locality no. 1, for example, locality no. 15 with its fossil fish from 3 to 5 million years ago. The so-called Upper Cave, above and south of locality no. 1, was found to contain the remains of modern humans, *homo sapiens,* and their artifacts. Under Pei Wenzhong, Jia Lanpo (1908–2001) and European collaborators like Franz Weidenreich and Teilhard de Chardin, the Zhoukoudian discoveries gained worldwide attention in the 1930s. Work was suspended in 1937 when the Japanese encroached on the Beijing region. As is well known, the original Peking Man fossils were lost in December, 1941, the early stages of the

Stage 1: Cave formation

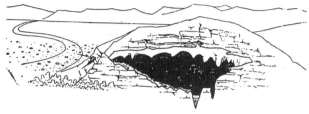

Stage 2: East entrance opens

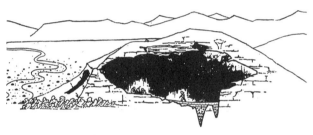

Stage 3: Initial hominid presence

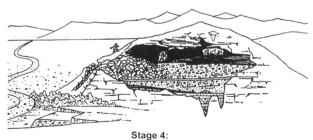

Stage 4:

East end collapse   West end hominid presence

Formation of the cave

Second World War, under mysterious circumstances that continue to stimulate speculation about their possible fate. Work resumed after Liberation, and a work station with display hall was erected.

The human fossils at Zhoukoudian locality no 1 were interpreted by the first generation of European and Chinese scholars as a "cave home" of early man. This human occupation was divided into three segments: the Lower Culture (levels 13–8) dated about 500,000–400,000 years ago; a Middle Culture (levels 7–6) of 400,000–300,000 years ago; and an Upper Culture (levels 5–1) of 300,000–200,000 years ago. (All of these segments fall into the Middle Pleistocene geologic epoch and the Lower Paleolithic. The Upper Cave, by contrast, is from the Upper Pleistocene and Upper Paleolithic.) The best known hominid fossils are crania, which are exceptionally thick, shaped like a tortoise carapace or cyclist's helmet according to some writers, and characterized by strong ridges front to back and across both the brow and the back of the skull. The brain capacity is 915–1225 cc, with an average of 1075 cc, which overlaps the lower range of modern humans (1000–1800 cc; average 1350 cc). In stature, these were individuals close to modern human size (males 156 cm, females 144 cm). Of twenty-two individuals that could be analyzed, fifteen (68%) died before age 14; only one lived over age 50. By 1939, Weidenreich and his colleagues had concluded these fossil humans were essentially identical to Java Man, now designated as *homo erectus*. The stone tools and animal bones suggested a hunting lifestyle, with large game from the plains being butchered and in some cases roasted around hearths inside the cave. Evidence of hackberries suggested the population also consumed this fruit. Weidenreich and others also suggested cannibalism based on the condition of the skulls, which were uniformly lacking their facial anatomy and had even been cut away around the base.

In the post-war decades, discoveries in Africa overshadowed work elsewhere on homo erectus. For their part, Chinese specialists were busy elsewhere in their country seeking new finds. Discoveries at Lantian, outside of Xi'an, and at Yuanmou, in Yunnan, pre-dated Zhoukoudian. Some finds of stone tools were even older, from the Lower Pleistocene. Recent work has also yielded important new erectus finds at Hexian, Anhui (c. 200,000 years ago), at Yunxian, Hubei (c. 730,000 years ago), and at Nanjing (c. 350,000 years ago). These finds and many others now offer much more data with which to contextualize the initial discoveries at Zhoukoudian. But, as is always true, they are a mixed bag: in some cases human fossils were found in isolation; in some cases they were associated with faunal remains or stone tools or both; the dating of finds varies in reliability; and findspots present various problems. The virtue of Dragon Bone Hill is its broad range of data, and these data have sparked rethinking of the conventional interpretations of the site.

Three major controversies surround contemporary discussions about Zhoukoudian: Was it a "cave home," did the population use fire, and was there cannibalism? Each debate hinges on the interpretation of specific pieces of physical evidence recovered from the site, some of it known only from casts and photographs of now lost fossils. The use of fire was first established early in the 1930s based on several kinds of evidence: black deposits identified as carbon; "hearths" found in some of the excavated layers; and burned and discolored fossil bone. The black deposits may not have been produced by fire it turns out, although they are carbon, and the so-called hearths in particular are now suspect. New studies of these features did not detect

Whose Home?

"Cave Home of Peking Man"

any phytoliths, the crystalline structures left by wood or other fuels. So the hearths have now been re-identified as silt, not accumulations of ash. Discolored bones seem to be the result of chemical changes occurring after the bone became fossil, but there do seem to be actual burned bones as well, which in turn suggests roasting meat to some specialists.

The debate about whether humans lived in the cave as well as the discussion of cannibalism both hinge largely on the condition of the human and animal fossils. As noted above, the crania are bereft of their facial anatomy, and most human bone recovered is badly broken. There are no complete skeletons, and some body parts are missing. The most persuasive analysis accounting for the condition of these fossils and the assortment of types is that the bones were accumulated by animal predators, especially a giant species of hyena that nested in the caves. (Their fossil bones and feces are both abundant.) Studies of marks on bone can discriminate under a microscope between an animal chewing and a stone tool cutting. Human fossils at Zhoukoudian carry marks from animals gnawing them, which would also account for such losses as the facial portions of skulls. Animal bones show tool marks over the traces of animal gnawing. This conjunction leads to the idea that *homo erectus* scavenged prey from other animal predators. Given the small size of most stone tools and the lack of weapons that could be used to hunt larger prey species, this makes some sense. Likewise, if *homo erectus* could utilize fire (perhaps only that occurring naturally) to scare off predators, either from a kill or from a cave shelter, they may have had an advantage compared to their ferocious animal rivals. Thus a picture of *homo erectus* as a scavenger who used fire and butchered purloined kills opportunistically in the cave has emerged. While human occupation of Locality 1 may have spanned 200,000 years, it now seems to have been intermittent, not a true cave home as often pictured. To complicate matters, tool marks on human skull parts suggest that *homo erectus* did deflesh human remains, even if most of the damage done to crania was actually the result of hyena predation.

Many other aspects of Peking Man have been reexamined since the first generation of scholars addressed these issues. It has been suggested, for example, that the extraordinarily thick skull was an adaptation to protect the enlarged brain from blunt trauma, literally head butting and violence within the species. The lack of hand axes, ubiquitous in Europe and Africa, has been explained as the result of characteristics of the materials available (mainly quartz), and/or other factors that obviated them, such as the use of perishable bamboo. Climate data suggest that Peking Man was actually a migratory species, moving south and north in response to interglacial fluctuations in the

temperature and moisture of the environment, possibly following game herds. Recent analyses have also
shifted the dates of the hominids at Zhoukoudian back
some 200,000 years to 670,000 to 410,000 years ago.

Outside China, many scholars are convinced that
homo erectus came out of Africa, or evolved in Africa and
Eurasia simultaneously, and over a million years later was
displaced by another species, *homo heidelbergensis*, which
also came out of Africa. Some Chinese scholars, however, hope to demonstrate a continuous evolution from
earlier species in Eurasia to Peking Man, and subsequently down to the modern populations of Eurasia. If
such long term continuity is endorsed, Peking Man
could be described as "Chinese." (There seems to be little dispute that Upper Cave Man, c. 18,000 years ago,
was fully modern *homo sapiens*.) The continual accumulation of new sites and new fossils will affect each of
these debates, just as more and more multi-disciplinary
and international collaboration regularly challenges
conventional wisdom. Retelling the story of Peking
Man—with or without his cave home—has just begun.

SUGGESTED
READING

One of the original Chinese excavators has written a
memoir of his work; see Jia Lanpo and Huang Weiwen,
The Story of Peking Man: From Archaeology to Mystery
(1990), illustrated with many historic photographs. J.
Gunnar Andersson's personal account is also worth
reading; *Children of the Yellow Earth* (1973). The loss of
the fossils is examined in Harry Shapiro, *Peking Man:
The Discovery, Disappearance and Mystery of a Priceless
Scientific Treasure* (1974). For an up-to-date overview of
the debates concerning Peking Man, see Noel T. Boaz
and Russell L. Ciochon, *Dragon Bone Hill: An Ice-Age
Saga of Homo Erectus* (2004).

Banpo: Farmers in the Loess Lands

2

BANPO MUSEUM
XI'AN, SHAANXI
YANGSHAO CULTURE, BANPO PHASE
C. 4800–4300 BCE

One of the strongest claims of archaeology—whether viewed as a branch of history, or of anthropology or, indeed, as a free-standing discipline—is its proven ability to create new knowledge. However archaeologists frame their goals and reason from their evidence, their practices generate new data with which to examine the human past. These data may be collections of broken, durable objects made by human hands (artifacts), or dry tables of statistics created by sampling, surveys, or laboratory analyses. The combination of archaeological techniques (stratigraphy, typology) and the natural sciences has been especially productive in the last half century, creating absolute datings, information on human ancestry, and sourcing resources in ways previously undreamed of. These data, in turn, allow archaeologists to create patterns in space and time.

At the mid-twentieth century, scholars in China had only the broadest and vaguest sense of prehistory. Finds were widely distributed in space and time, the few excavations were small in scale, interpretations were simplistic (for example, painted pottery vs. black

Interior at Banpo Museum

pottery), and datings were highly subjective. The first systematic steps to chart the development of human societies before the Bronze Age in China Proper were taken in a series of excavations during the 1950s, none more influential than a site called Banpo, on the eastern edge of Xi'an. The prehistoric settlement at Banpo was the first instance in modern Chinese archaeology of an extensive excavation that targeted an entire human community, its dwellings, craft production, and burials. Much influenced by Soviet "material culture" studies (as a program for archaeological research) and ethnographic analysis, the current senior generation of Chinese archaeologists created a multi-faceted picture of a "primitive commune." The site has been preserved as a museum, both for its own importance and as an introduction to prehistory generally. While its attractions are modest when compared to the terra cotta warriors in trenches further to the east, Banpo tells us much both about the past and about our capacity to rediscover it.

crock itself, one commonly associated with serving
and eating food, and hence a object put in a different
functional context than its maker first intended.
Distinguishing the different or multiple uses of objects
over their life cycle is a necessary complement to their
typological classification. Merging data about prove-
nance (where something is found), typology (form,
suggesting fabrication techniques as well as usage), and
contents in the aggregate has created much of our
knowledge of the past. Looting or natural destruction,
which destroy these data, are therefore the bane of an
archaeologist's existence.

When J.G. Andersson and Li Ji first reported
sherds of painted pottery from Henan (Yangshao),
Shanxi (Xiyincun), and the Gansu corridor (Banshan,
Machang) in the 1920s, they had little comparative
material, much less stratigraphy or dating techniques,
to help interpret their finds. Excavations like Banpo,
and its many successors over the last half century, lead
us to place the finds of the 1920s in the latter part of

Reconstructed house,
Banpo Museum

Banpo pottery

the Middle Neolithic Yangshao Culture, but later in absolute date than Banpo and the phase it now represents. The painted ceramics found at all these sites are low-fired earthenwares, formed by hand rather than on a wheel, and baked in oxygen-rich kilns producing a reddish paste. The pots are easily broken and permeable by water. Surfaces are generally burnished when the clay is still soft with a smooth stone or shell. Slip is normally applied after firing. At Banpo the designs are usually brown-black (rich in iron), and motifs include a variety of geometric forms, a few animals, and a mysterious "mask." Simple as these designs may be, they are the beginnings of Chinese pictorial art.

Village Societies

The processes by which the Banpo site was excavated and recorded created a catalogue of the preserved material culture of that ancient community. These archaeological processes have been re-enacted thousands of times at locales spread across China Proper.

Wedded with stratigraphy and dating techniques, these innumerable experiments at punching a hole into the past have constructed the picture we have today of human societies since the last Ice Age. Not surprisingly, many of our generalizations are akin to abstract statements made about humans on other continents.

TABLE 1
SIMPLIFIED CHRONOLOGY OF
NEOLITHIC SITES

Early Neolithic   c. 10,000–7500 BCE
    Xushui (Hebei) and Wannian Cave (Jiangxi)

Middle Neolithic   c. 7500–5000 BCE
    Cishan (Hebei)
    Peiligang (Henan)
    Houli (Shandong)
    Pengtoushan (Hunan)
    Xinglongwa (Inner Mongolia)

Late Neolithic   c. 5000–3000 BCE
    Yangshao (Henan, Shanxi, Shaanxi)
    Dawenkou (Shandong)
    Majiayao (Gansu)
    Chujialing (Hubei)
    Hemudu (Zhejiang)
    Hongshan (Liaoning, Inner Mongolia)

Terminal Neolithic   c. 3000–2000 BCE
    Taosi (Shanxi)
    Longshan (Shandong)
    Shijiahe (Hubei)
    Liangzhu (Zhejiang)

Mask design on painted pottery

Over this long span, human groups moved from hunting and gathering to dependence on cultivating plants and domesticated animals, farming. Village life as farmers has dominated human history in China, as elsewhere, for most of the last 10 to 12,000 years; farmers still predominate among the Chinese population. Only about 4 to 6,000 years ago did larger communities emerge in the archaeological record and with them more complex societies. Such a complex society is featured at Liangzhu, in Hangzhou, Zhejiang (Ch. 3). Even during the Bronze Age after the emergence of chiefdoms and the state, the majority of the population remained village dwellers, not urbanites, and farmers, not craft workers, warriors, or kings.

Many sites of the early, middle, and late Neolithic have been preserved in China (Table 1). A number are open for visits as site museums, and most local and provincial museums also display their regional Neolithic heritage. The basics of archaeological practice and reasoning summarized above are equally applicable to understanding all these sites. What changes from site to site is the adaptation of an ancient community to its local environment. At Hemudu, a late Neolithic (c. 5000–3300 BCE) community on the southern shores of Hangzhou Bay (Yuyao, Zhejiang), stilt houses in the shallows were favored, and resources from the estuary were exploited. Neolithic cultures across the loess lands predictably have much in common with Banpo (for example, Dahecun, Zhengzhou, Henan), but cave dwellings are found in parts of Shaanxi and Gansu (like Dadiwan, Datong, Gansu). In the south, rock shelters (like Zengpiyan, Guilin, Guangxi) were exploited and a different agricultural subsistence—paddy rice—was developed. Stone dwellings are found in the steppe zones north of the Great Wall, such as Xinglongwa (Chifeng, Inner Mongolia).

A new general introduction to Chinese prehistory is badly needed; twenty years on, K.C. Chang's *The Archaeology of Ancient China,* 4th ed. (1986) has not been replaced. See also Chang Kwang-chih and Xu Pingfang, *The Formation of Chinese Civilization: An Archaeological Perspective* (2005), especially the chapter by Zhang Zhongpei on "The Yangshao Period." Entries in Xiaoneng Yang, *The Golden Age of Chinese Archaeology* (1999) are also helpful.

SUGGESTED READING

3 Liangzhu: An Age of Jade

LIANGZHU CULTURE MUSEUM
HANGZHOU, ZHEJIANG
C. 3000–2200 BCE

Like other archaeologists, Chinese scholars experience booms. The excitement surrounding discovery of Liangzhu jade artifacts peaked in the 1980s and 90s. This Neolithic culture, first defined by its black pottery in the 1930s, had been designated as a regional archaeological culture as early as 1960. Liangzhu sites are distributed throughout the Lower Yangzi macroregion (modern Shanghai, Jiangsu, and Zhejiang); the type site is near a village northwest of Hangzhou. From the outset, Liangzhu finds were understood as a culture akin to the classic Longshan of Shandong. But expert opinion in an era before carbon 14 datings placed Liangzhu in a much later chronological position than the Longshan, perhaps the late Zhou or even Han periods (5th–1st centuries BCE). Buttressing this guess was the view that jades associated with Liangzhu sites could not be prehistoric. Indeed, such objects as *cong* cylinders were identified as archaistic Ming-period (1368–1644) creations, not authentic prehistoric jades.

Several stratified sites placing Liangzhu levels and jades in the prehistoric period, subsequently supported

by absolute datings, were published in the 1980s. The
sites were cemeteries, and several outside Hangzhou
attracted attention for the sheer quantity of jade
objects, sometimes thousands of pieces in a single
modest grave. These beautiful jades have been extensively reproduced; their classic forms and intricate
iconography account for much of the cachet of this
subject. Settlements, unfortunately, remained almost
unknown, and only in the last decade has this situation
begun to change. The breakthrough and now main
focus of excavations in Zhejiang has been the "site
cluster" (*yizhi qun*) northwest of the Liangzhu type
site. At its nucleus is a raised terrace on the scale of a
large walled site, named Mojiao Shan. If the Liangzhu
Culture was a complex society—a chiefdom or incipient state—the Mojiao Shan nexus would be the leading candidate for its center.

Yaoshan altar

Neolithic Chiefdoms

The Liangzhu people inhabited a salubrious ecological niche in the Lower Yangzi macroregion, bounded on the north by that river and on the south by the Qiantang River flowing into Hangzhou Bay. Lake Tai, the "great lake," occupies the "eye" of this delta, and may have been even larger than today. Mild climate, alluvial soils, and abundant moisture created an agricultural economy praised in historic times as the "land of rice and silk," two resources that were already known to the Liangzhu Culture. East of Lake Tai between the two rivers, however, dry ground was at a premium. The Liangzhu people congregated on low natural mounds (most only 2 to 3 m above sea level), building them up with thousands of baskets of soil carried on their backs. Liangzhu sites—residential, altars, and cemeteries—are always associated with such mounds. While several hundred finds are now recorded in the Lower Yangzi region as a whole, only a fraction are reported, most only in brief accounts. Radiocarbon datings place this thriving culture in the third millennium, from c. 3000 to 2200 BCE.

Northwest of Hangzhou in Yuhang County are more than 100 sites scattered across the countryside in an area about 8 km east-west by 3 km north-south. The greatest concentration is north of a highway connecting the small towns of Liangzhu and Pingyao, southeast of the Zhaoxi, a river flowing from the southwest to the north and east. Sites are also found north of this stream in the low hills of the Tianmu Mountains, covered today by fir trees and tea bushes. The entire area is under intense population pressure. Several major discoveries came after local residents built new houses on high ground (actually ancient mounds) and looted objects uncovered when digging the foundations.

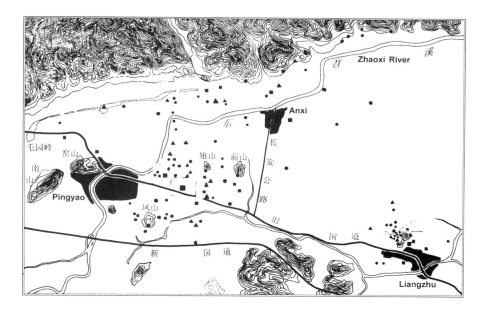

On the highway between Liangzhu and Pingyao stretches the artificial raised terrace called Mojiao Shan. Although only portions have been probed and little excavated, its dimensions are known to be about 670 m east-west and 450 m north-south. The terrace is the cumulative result of extensive earthmoving. Some margins are bounded by an adobe and pounded-earth wall. The top of the terrace is 5 to 8 m above surrounding terrain, and has patches of pounded earth as well as post holes. A huge timber recovered from the base of the terrace may have been a beam used in a large structure. Three raised platforms were built on the terrace, perhaps altars or foundations of large timber structures. The 300 hectares (300,000 sq m) occupied by the Mojiao Shan site are comparable to some of the largest walled prehistoric sites in the Yellow River drainage. The four corners of Mojiao shan are occupied by cemetery plots, including one of the richest, Fanshan on the northwest.

Map of Liangzhu site cluster

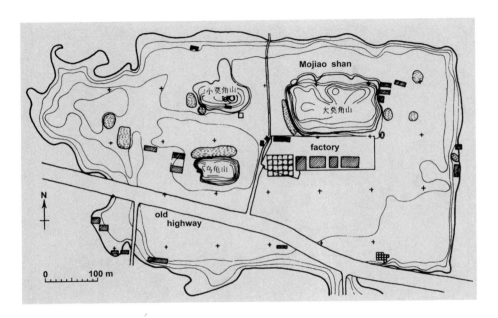

Mojiao shan

小莫角山

大莫角山

factory

N

old
highway

0   100 m

Plan of Mojiao Shan

The finds that drove the Liangzhu boom of the 1980s, however, were small cemeteries on less imposing earthen mounds. The first, Fanshan, excavated in 1986, contained eleven graves arrayed in two rows, north and south. Its seven large burials held over 3200 jade items (1100 groups) including the largest and most distinctive examples of the *cong* cylinder and *yue* axe ever recovered. A second site found in 1987, Yaoshan, is about 5 km northeast of Fanshan, on a natural hill itself about 35 m in elevation. Here archaeologists uncovered a well-preserved earthen altar, about 20 m square. Different colors of earth were massed together: a central square of red soil about 7 m by 6 m, a band of gray soil about 2 m wide bordering it, and an outer zone of yellow-brown soil covered with gravel on north, west, and south. Twelve burials were arrayed in north and south rows, the graves clearly postdating the altar construction. Another altar-burial site, located in 1990, was excavated at Huiguan Shan, some 2 km west of Fanshan. The altar there measured about 45 m east–west by 33 m north–south. It again had a trench of gray fill surrounding a central zone some 7 m by 9 m. Only four burials, all badly looted, were found. It is believed that more burials originally existed on this mound, because of the large quantities of jades recovered by Public Security from residents of this area.

Like the contemporaneous Longshan Culture of Shandong, the Liangzhu Culture stood at the threshold of civilization (see Table 1). This society supported a densely occupied center, although apparently without a walled core site. In addition to the massive earthworks at Mojiao Shan, surveys have located several areas where sites run together with areas of 1 to 6 hectares. For example, twenty sites cluster within a 1-km radius of Liangzhu. A few of these (like Miaoqian) have yielded houses and water wells and other finds indicative of residential use. Most find-spots, however, are less than a hectare in size. In addition, a man-made dike or levee some 4 km in length runs east–west at some distance from the foothills of the mountains to the north. This may have provided flood protection against runoff from that direction. A major component of this culture that still remains under-represented in the archaeological record is workshops, both for pottery production and jade working.

A Jade Age?

The quantity, range of specialized types, and exacting surface decoration make Liangzhu jades a fascinating topic. Jades of these kinds, including the distinctive *cong* cylinder and *bi* disk, were well known to pre-modern antiquarians, who of course could not place them in space or time. The appropriation of the *cong* cylinder shape by potters of the imperial kilns near Hangzhou during the Southern Song period (1127–1279; see Ch. 22), demonstrates their appreciation by antiquarian scholars. *Bi* disks were also made in considerable quantities in late Zhou and Han times, possibly also a reaction to the discovery of these Neolithic objects. Moreover, the modern documentation of these jade forms in archaeological cultures as far afield as Shanxi, Sichuan, and Guangdong argues for a wide exchange network in prehistoric times.

Consider first the quantities unearthed. The Fanshan site, with merely eleven burials—one damaged and another without a proper trench—yielded 3200 hard-stones, from minute beads to a massive *cong* weighing 6.5 kg. Fanshan grave no. 23 had fifty-four *bi* disks, an all-time high for this one type. Grave no. 20 was inventoried at 547 hard-stones, a number that explodes when individual pieces within groups are counted separately. The implications of these numbers are remarkable: (1) Raw material was obviously in good supply. The hard-stones probably came from local sources (not Central Asia), of which a site near Liyang, Jiangsu, west of Lake Tai is currently the best known. (2) Several centers must have produced the jades, which then circulated across a broad area. While the characteristic stone of Fanshan and Yaoshan is a milky white color, other centers in Shanghai and Jiangsu exploited different minerals. (3) Individuals evidently amassed large numbers of these objects, which were then interred in a burial. For every undisturbed grave with hundreds of beads and other types on its earthen floor, we should probably imagine a cohort of the peers of the deceased similarly dressed for the occasion.

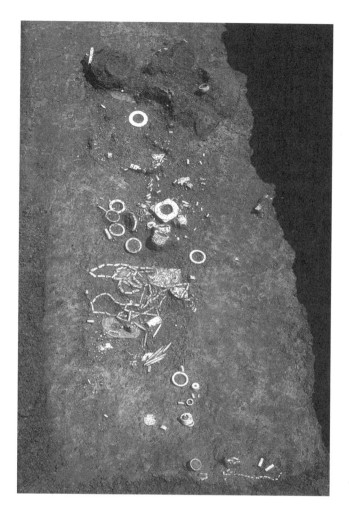

Jades in grave no. 7, Yaoshan

Consider also function. Jades were a part of personal adornment for both men and women, and probably also tokens to be manipulated in symbolic rituals. The many plaques (*fu* or *guan*) and awl-shaped forms found near skulls may have been used in elaborate headdresses worn by both men and women. They may have been similar to the feathered headdress that surmount the "spirit emblem" motif. Hard-stone flat axes (*yue*), on the other hand, while close in form to useable stone axes, were hafted on handles inlaid with small specks of stone and given hard-stone finials and butts. They most probably were carried as tokens of rank. *Cong* cylinders may be limited to male burials. *Bi* disks, while obviously analogous with spindle whorls associated with women, were so large and heavy as to be beyond practical application. Like the cylinders they must have been symbolic tokens.

Consider finally decoration. The iconography of these jades has stimulated much discussion; it allows every author a wide-open field for speculation. Liangzhu iconography has been tied in particular to shamanism known ethnographically in various Asian and Pacific-rim cultures. Shamans are intermediaries

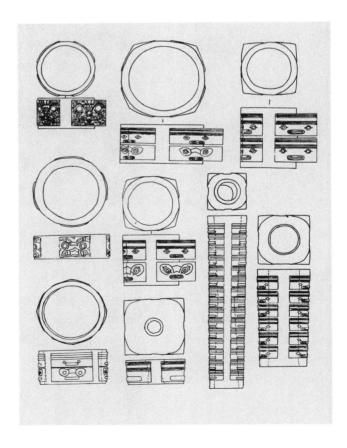

Cong types

between this world and another, between men and spirits. Animals often aid shamans as their "familiars." Masks are frequently important gear for a shaman's performance, including out-of-body travel and communication with spirits. Liangzhu jades indeed are strong on facial or mask designs, sometimes with animal attributes like fangs. The most elaborate type of image (the "spirit emblem") combines a human-like figure above with an animal-like mask below. This complex rendering is relatively rare, but simplified versions derived from it are pervasive among all jade types. The rudimentary face (merely eyes, nose, and jaws) could represent a spirit or the shaman's mask. The figure bestriding the face/mask could be the shaman, perhaps with mask and head gear. Possession of these stones could mark the individuals buried at Fanshan and elsewhere as shamans. Although widely invoked by scholars today, a shamanistic interpretation is only one possibility given present evidence.

"Spirit emblem" design

The archaeological evidence for the Liangzhu Culture indicates a stratified society. An elite enjoyed specialized luxury crafts, both burnished black earthenwares with minute, incised decoration, and a great profusion of jades, albeit without any traces as yet of metal. Rudimentary signs found on some pottery may represent a formative stage before proper writing. The main contrasts between the Liangzhu and Longshan Cultures hinge on local environment and resources. Yet while the Longshan Cultures can be seen as precursors to the Shang and their Bronze Age peers in North China, the Liangzhu Culture by contrast remains exotic, especially when examined through the lens of its jades.

The sites near Hangzhou have parallels in other regions, but so far no cluster like that surrounding Mojiao Shan is known. In rural Shanghai burials were found around a raised mound at Fuquan Shan. Similar sites are known at Sidun, near Changzhou, Jiangsu, and at Zhaoling Shan, near Kunshan, Jiangsu. Displays of Liangzhu jades from these sites will be found in the Shanghai Museum and the Nanjing Museum.

SUGGESTED READING   Shao Wangping, "The Formation of Civilization," in Chang Kwang-chih and Xu Pingfang, *The Formation of Chinese Civilization: An Archaeological Perspective* (2005) covers much of this territory from an historical perspective. Liu Li's more detailed and scholarly *The Chinese Neolithic: Trajectories to Early States* (2004) focuses on the development of complex societies using anthropological theory. A selection of Liangzhu jades is published in Xiaoneng Yang, *The Golden Age of Chinese Archaeology* (1999).

Xia, Shang, and Zhou

(1900–221 BCE)

In pre-modern tradition history began with the "Three Dynasties:" Xia, Shang, and Zhou. Sima Qian begins his reign-by-reign annals and royal genealogies in the *Records of the Grand Historian* (*Shi ji, c.* 100 BCE) starting with the Xia kings. In Sima Qian's view, the Xia were the fountainhead of a line of legitimate dynastic succession that extended through the Shang, Zhou, and Qin to the Han, his own day. In his accounts, Sima Qian observed a cyclical process in which a virtuous man founded a new royal line only to have that line fail due to the behavior of a despicable descendant. A new dynasty (first the Shang, and then the Zhou) then claimed Heaven's Mandate to rule because of their own virtue. Their case was buttressed by lurid stories of the excesses of the wicked last ruler of the previous ruling house and by inspiring, heroic actions of the founder. In Sima Qian and the commentaries appended to his work, the Three Dynasties were also associated with different regions: Xia in the center of North China (western Henan and Shanxi), Shang to the east (Shandong-Hebei), and Zhou to the west (Shaanxi).

Many contemporary Chinese scholars have invested great energy in identifying archaeological sites as the capitals of these dynasties named in received sources. Most Chinese archaeologists believe that a site called Erlitou near Luoyang was for a time a

Xia capital. If one takes the traditional commentaries and texts seriously, Erlitou was certainly at the right place and the right time to be a Xia capital. The identification of Anyang (Ch. 4) with Late Shang kings is in fact secure; where earlier Shang kings named by Sima Qian may have held forth, however, continues to elicit lively debate. The leading contenders are two large walled sites in Henan at modern Zhengzhou and Yanshi. Likewise, areas linked to the Zhou people and contemporary with the Late Shang kings have been investigated in the Wei River valley of modern Shaanxi. This region is known by tradition as the "plain of Zhou" (Ch. 6, Zhou Yuan). It is west of Xi'an near the Famen Si (Ch. 19) in Qishan and Fufeng counties. The royal Zhou dynastic capitals, named Feng and Hao after rivers west of Xi'an, are not as well known, although extensive cemeteries have been excavated. Thus even if one remains agnostic about the Erlitou question, two of the Three Dynasties capitals can be studied today through a judicious blend of historiographic, epigraphic, and archaeological evidence.

All of these archaeological cultures were Bronze Age societies, by which we mean that they used this alloy for various tools, weapons, chariot fittings, and most of all ritual vessels and musical bells. Although metals were exploited by 2000 BCE (or even earlier) in several regional Neolithic cultures, significant use of bronze alloy in North China starts at Erlitou, and reaches its first high point in the late second millennium. Casting bronze is extremely widespread in the first millennium across most of north and central China. However, for scholars of anthropology and history, the Chinese Bronze Age is more aptly described as an age of early states that controlled fairly large territories with powerful rulers (kings) who administered their lands and subjects through at least a proto-bureaucracy. Complex chiefdoms or incipient states may have emerged even before the appearance of bronze casting (Ch. 3, Liangzhu), but in general state-level societies were a Bronze Age phenomenon in most parts of China Proper.

The definitive treatment of the Chinese Bronze Age is M. Loewe and E.L. Shaughnessy, eds., *The Cambridge History of Ancient China: From the Origins of Civilization to 221 B.C.* (1999). See also Chang Kwang-chih and Xu Pingfang, *The Formation of Chinese Civilization: An Archaeological Perspective* (2005).

SUGGESTED READING

4 Anyang: The "Ruins of Yin"

ANYANG WORK STATION AND YINXU BOWUYUAN
ANYANG, HENAN
SHANG PERIOD, C. 1250–1046 BCE
WORLD HERITAGE SITE

When they were surveyed in 1999, professional archaeologists in China voted the campaigns at Anyang, which began in 1928, the most important archaeological work of the twentieth century. The rationale behind this high esteem is not hard to fathom. Anyang marks the beginnings of true history in East Asia with the recovery of the earliest primary historical sources. Anyang was indubitably a capital of the second of the Three Dynasties, the Shang, with

Restored palace at Yinxu Archaeology Park

many kinds of unambiguous evidence to sustain that identification. And with Anyang, archaeology as practiced by Chinese scholars first came into its own, unearthing in impressive detail a complex Bronze Age civilization that confirmed long-standing traditions.

The region surrounding Anyang on the northern border of Henan had been known to scholars as the "ruins of Yin" (Yinxu) for many centuries. In the Northern Song (960–1126) period, it had been a rich source of the bronze ritual vessels esteemed in antiquarian scholarship. And at the turn of the twentieth century, a village near Anyang was identified as the source of "dragon bones" used in traditional medicine that bore archaic graphs, ancient Chinese script better known as "oracle-bone" writing. In fact, the discovery of these writings led Chinese archaeologists to explore the cotton fields near Xiaotun in 1928. The young

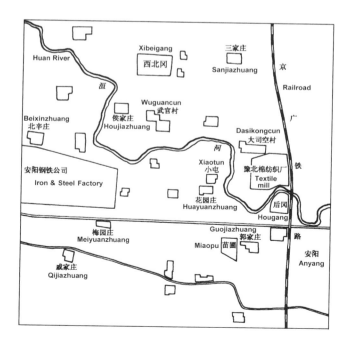

Map of Yinxu

scholar who took on this task, Dong Zuobin, confirmed that many fields showed evidence of bones and
shells being dug up. By October of that year, Dong
had made his first harvest, and he reported the site
deserved further exploration. Over the next decade,
the newly established Academia Sinica put its Archaeology Section to work in fifteen seasons (1928–37) on
both sides of the Huan River northwest of Anyang.
Their discoveries—palatial foundations, royal tombs,
deposits of inscribed bones and shells, and numerous
bronze ritual vessels, weapons, and chariot fittings—
sketched the outlines of a large Bronze Age settlement
occupied by the last kings of the Shang. Members of
the excavation staff, especially Li Ji, Dong Zuobin, Hu
Houxuan, and Xia Nai, went on to shape the development of archaeological theory and practice in
twentieth-century China. Their achievements at the
"ruins of Yin" laid the groundwork for all Bronze Age
archaeology.

A Bronze Age
Ceremonial
Center

A visit to Anyang and Yinxu today begins with a drive
to the Archaeological Park (Yinxu Bowuyuan) northeast of Xiaotun on high ground above the Huan
River, a kilometer from the rail station. With a population of some 600,000, the district of Anyang is no
longer the sleepy, remote county seat of the 1920s and
30s. The Archaeological Park protects the palace district, where over fifty pounded-earth foundations
were unearthed in the early 1930s. These finds resulted
from a learning process. Opening long strip trenches,
the excavators came upon extremely dense deposits of
soil. Only as they enlarged the trenches and traced the
outlines of these deposits did the excavators realize
they could not be flood sediments as was first sup-

posed. The regular shapes, sharp corners, and occasional rows of river cobbles on the surfaces at intervals near the margins led to the conclusion these were man-made earthen blocks that had supported timber-frame structures. Several of these halls have been reconstructed at the site with thatched roofs, carved and painted wooden pillars, and whitewashed mud-plaster walls. Over the period of the last Shang kings, from Wu Ding onwards, this concentration of buildings served the kings, perhaps as residences, certainly for sacrifice and divination. The palaces were hemmed in on north and east by the bend of the river. Work since the 1960s has also traced a large ditch running from the river on the north toward the south making a right angle bend to enter the river again on the east. Thus the palace district was entirely enclosed by a dry ditch or water channel and the river.

Many of the most important discoveries at Yinxu have been made within this precinct. On the last day of work in season thirteen (1936), Li Ji uncovered a block of shells that had to be removed as a single mass. This pit, YH127, held 17,000 inscribed shells from the reign of Wu Ding. In the early 1970s, another major find south of Xiaotun village produced about 5,000 bones and shells, while in 1991 another excavation east of the village yielded 1500 more. These three find-spots account for the great majority of the excavated oracle-bone inscriptions that scholars study today. In the southwest corner of the Archaeological Park stands a statue of the royal consort Lady Hao and a re-creation of her tomb and its offering hall. Her burial, dug in 1976, was the first unlooted royal grave to be opened at Anyang. Her name was found on about half of the 200 bronzes in the tomb; some 150 references to her activities in the oracle-bone inscriptions document her status as a royal consort of King Wu Ding. Thus Lady Hao is the earliest historical personage in Chinese history whose material legacy has been found.

Across the river from the park is a display hall devoted to the royal tombs, usually known by their locale, Xibeigang ("northwest ridge.") Like the palace district, this is high ground, today mostly open fields. The exhibition here displays a tract of sacrificial pits in rows near several large tombs at the east end of the cemetery. These tombs were first excavated in fall, 1934, and for three seasons became the hub of activity at Anyang, employing hundreds of workers. Two clusters of large shaft burials were cleared, eight of

Rendering by Yang Hongxun of tomb no. 5 temple.

them with four ramps each. With depths of 10 to 13 m and chambers as large as 10 by 6 m at their bases, these tombs were quickly identified as the resting places of the Shang kings. But the tombs had been thoroughly pillaged; one tunnel was 21 by 18 m across at ground level. Only deposits tucked away in the corners outside the main chambers were recovered in 1934–35 (see Introduction, p. 18); hence the importance of the intact tomb of Lady Hao. Although much smaller and lacking ramps, that burial, with hundreds of bronzes and jades, intimated the large quantities of wealth that could have been placed in the royal tombs.

Over the nearly eighty years of work at Anyang, the extent of the excavations has expanded outwards in all directions. The total area is now estimated at about 30 sq km straddling both sides of the river. The most numerous finds across this landscape have been cemeteries, especially south and west of Xiaotun village. Most of these cemeteries consist of clusters of burials that apparently belonged to lineages of non-royal status. Some of these clusters have chariot burials, which were also found near the palace-temple foundations. The Work Station of the Institute of Archaeology, Beijing, is located just west of Xiaotun, and has a fine display of artifacts from hundreds of digs in and around Anyang conducted since the 1950s including a well-preserved chariot pit. In addition to several thousand graves, the Work Station's teams have uncovered residential areas and workshops, including a large bronze-casting site southeast of Xiaotun village at Miaopu North.

A site so important and accorded such sustained attention would seem an unlikely venue for unexpected discoveries. Yet this was precisely what hap-

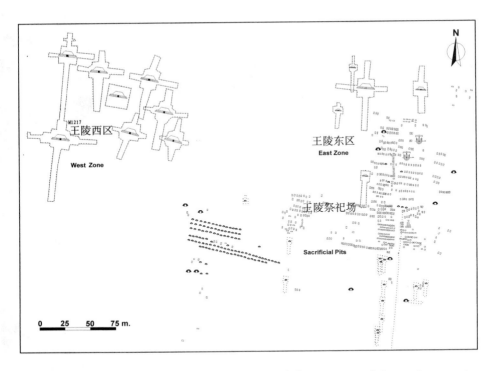

Plan of royal tombs, Xibeigang

pened in 1998–99, while a survey of the region was in progress. Opening trial trenches north of the river between the villages of Huayuanzhuang and Sanjiazhuang, the Work Team encountered segments of a wall, which proved to be a square compound almost 2 km on a side. The wall was dated to the period immediately prior to the first kings who divined at Anyang, now referred to as the "Middle Shang" period. Happily most of this previously unsuspected city site is open terrain, much of it an airfield. Additional prospecting quickly located a cluster of two dozen foundations. One of these, unearthed in 2001, was a courtyard 175 m across and 90 m deep, the largest architectural site from the early Bronze Age. The Huan-bei ("north of the Huan River") Shang wall is now one of a handful of major Shang sites in Henan that predate the historic occupation of Anyang,

providing important evidence for earlier phases of
Shang civilization.

It was obvious to all observers in the 1930s that the civilization identified at Anyang could not be the beginning of the Bronze Age in China. The roots of its
characteristic features, such as writing or bronze casting,
awaited discovery. The apparent mystery Anyang posed
led to speculation about connections with cultures outside China (diffusion), about the identity of the Zhou
who eventually conquered Shang (barbarians?), and
about the historicity of the first of the Three Dynasties,
the Xia. The last fifty years have seen all of these mys-
teries clarified by major discoveries across North China.

    Earlier phases of the culture manifest at Anyang
were recognized at other sites in Henan in the 1950s.
The major find was near Zhengzhou, where a large
walled city site was documented under the historic,
Ming-period walls. Most parts of this "early Shang"
center have been difficult to investigate because the
modern city lies atop. However, sections of the Shang
wall are visible above ground and have been preserved,
and palace foundations as well as graves with bronzes
are now known in quantity. The Henan Museum is an
excellent introduction to these important discoveries.
In the late 1960s, and continuing in the 1970s, efforts
east of Luoyang (Ch. 13) by the Institute of
Archaeology, unearthed a large settlement even earlier
than Zhengzhou named after the village of Erlitou.
Most Chinese scholars now equate this site and its culture with the Xia. The type site is extensive, with many
compounds, evidence of bronze casting, and rich
graves. The palace core here was walled, but no exterior wall on a scale like Zhengzhou has yet been

The Roots of Shang Civilization

found. The site itself is not normally open to visitors, but the Luoyang Museum offers good displays. In the 1980s, another large walled site was found east of Erlitou across the Luo River near the Yanshi county seat. This center had massive walls on a par with Zhengzhou, and also several walled palatial compounds; like Huan-bei, to the benefit of the archaeologists much of the site remains open fields. Identification of this site has shifted back and forth between various Shang and Xia capitals in recent years; the current consensus favors the inception of Shang for its dating. Thus when sites in Henan are taken into account, a trajectory from the early Bronze Age at Erlitou (Xia?) through the early (Yanshi and Zhengzhou), middle (Huan-bei), and late Shang (Anyang) can be established.

However, these discoveries do not complete the present picture of the early Bronze Age. Lesser centers have been found in several other regions: to the north in Hebei (Taixi in Gaocheng county, east of Shijiazhuang), to the east in Shandong (Daxinzhuang, outside Ji'nan), to the south in Hubei (Panlongcheng, north of Wuhan), and to the west in the Wei River valley (Laoniupo, east of Xi'an). Most scholars conclude that these sites delimit the rough outlines of a Shang cultural horizon during the mid-late second millennium BCE. Other peoples using bronze coexisted with these settlements, and interacted with them (Ch. 5, Sanxingdui).

Artifacts looted from Anyang in earlier periods, or even during the first excavations, are among the highlights of many collections. Several American, European, and Japanese collections hold Anyang

Animal mask design (taotie)

objects, notably, the Freer–Sackler Gallery (Washington D.C.), Nelson-Atkins Museum (Kansas City), Asian Art Museum (San Francisco), British Museum (London), and Nezu Institute of Arts (Tokyo). Objects properly excavated from Anyang in the 1930s are on display in the National Palace Museum, Taibei; Academia Sinica (Taiwan), which sponsored those digs, also displays some of its holdings. The foremost collections of ritual bronzes in China are the Shanghai Museum, where the permanent galleries offer an intensive course on the subject, and the Shaanxi History Museum (Xi'an). The National Museum (formerly History Museum) on Tian'anmen Square, Beijing, also offers a useful overview.

The most up-to-date introduction to all aspects of Anyang is Robert L. Thorp, *China in the Early Bronze Age: Shang Civilization* (2005), pp. 117–213. Chapters in *The Cambridge History of Ancient China* (1999) by David N. Keightley and Robert W. Bagley are also recommended. Li Ji's *Anyang* (1977) is a memoir of the prewar excavations by the principal figure involved.

SUGGESTED READING

5 Sanxingdui: Another Bronze Age

SANXINGDUI MUSEUM
GUANGHAN, SICHUAN
C. 1600–1050 BCE

Bronze standing figure from pit no. 2

Chinese scholars have been diligent in fitting together received historical traditions and new archaeological discoveries. Analysis of early Bronze Age sites, most in Henan province (Ch. 4), produced satisfying correlations. The oracle-bones recovered at Anyang explicitly linked that site complex with the late Shang kings, while a variety of early textual sources have encouraged scholars to propose plausible (if not certain) identifications for the walls at Yanshi and Zhengzhou, and the palaces at Erlitou. It can be said that in North China history has often been a credible guide to where to look and what might be found.

But some archaeological finds are not predicted by historical traditions, and a major discovery may confound conventional wisdom. No find of the pre-imperial period fulfills this description more aptly than a site north of Chengdu: Sanxingdui. Like most excavations, the finds at "three star mounds" were named after a local place. Additional work across the Chengdu Basin has since encouraged archaeologists to take this dig as the type site for a culture that flourished from the middle through the late second millennium BCE. The walls built south of the Yazi River

delimit an area about 1800 by 2000 m, making this site
about the size of the inner wall at Zhengzhou or the
newly-found Huan-bei wall at Anyang. But no one
would confuse the material culture in evidence at this
site with Henan finds of the same era. Sanxingdui
seems to represent an alternative early Bronze Age
culture within modern-day China, a tradition quite
foreign to the expectations of conventional wisdom.

Recognition of the Sanxingdui Culture has a modern
history. Finds of hard-stones and jades were first noted
in Guanghan, about 40 km north of Chengdu, in the
1920s. Many stone blades and rings were dispersed
from several pits opened at that time, but their context
remained obscure. Regional surveys performed in the
1960s and 70s identified segments of the ancient wall,
and investigations in the 1970s and 80s reported distinctive pottery and traces of houses. But real attention
did not come until the summer of 1986, when workers at a brick factory digging clay from an embank-
ment opened a pit full of wonderful things. Called to
the find, provincial archaeologists gazed on a rich
deposit of ivory, hard-stones, and bronzes. As excavation of the first pit went forward, a second pit nearby
was discovered at the brick works. It held similar contents, and like the first, seemed unlikely to be a burial.
These twin discoveries have been designated sacrificial
pits, although the usual markers of sacrifice known
from northern sites are not present. The inevitable
consequence of any major find is additional survey
and probing, both around the find spot and in the
region. Since the late 1980s, the roots of the
Sanxingdui Culture have been traced both at the type
site and at a half dozen even earlier walled sites in the

An Exotic
Culture

Chengdu Basin. At the same time, more features within the Sanxingdui wall have also been explored. A major museum of these finds on the site opened a few years ago, and recently doubled its exhibition space. Sanxingdui is now a major attraction for anyone interested in Chinese archaeology.

The walled site surrounding the museum is much larger than any walls from the preceding local Baodun Culture. The Sanxingdui walls were built in period II, roughly comparable to the late occupation of Erlitou or early Erligang in Henan (Ch. 4). As wide as 40 m at its base and 20 m at its top level, the wall enclosed zones devoted to high-status structures, several kinds of workshops, and the sacrificial pits, with graves so far only in areas outside the wall. While this site was abandoned in the early Western Zhou period, the culture clearly survived in the area of Chengdu. Two sites there—Shi'erqiao and Jinsha—have strong links to the type site, and carry the development of this culture forward into the Western Zhou and even beyond. Jinsha in particular has been extraordinarily rich in

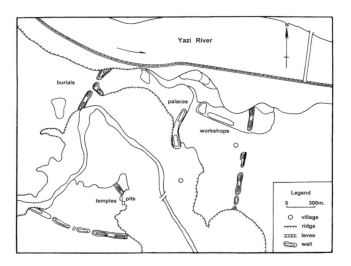

Plan of Sanxingdui

attractive hard-stones and artifacts of bronze and gold reminiscent of Sanxingdui. Jinsha will likely become a major archaeological destination in the near future.

The two pits at Sanxingdui were simple excavations of modest scale. Pit no. 1 was a rectangle about 4.5 by 3.5 m, barely a meter and a half deep. Three short ramps led to the base, which was slightly smaller than the opening. Pit no. 2, about 30 m to the northwest, was even simpler and, from stratigraphy, according to some accounts slightly later in date. It was a rectangle 5.3 by 2.3 m with a similar depth. Together the two pits held hundreds of objects: about 900 items of bronze, over 600 jades and hard-stones, various stone, ceramic, and gold artifacts, plus eighty ivory tusks and more than 4600 cowries. These objects may have been laid in the pits in a sequence rather that randomly disposed; many, however, were broken. Some animal remains and the ivory tusks had apparently been burned, the main justification for classifying the finds as sacrificial pits.

The most striking of all these artifacts are the staring faces of bronze masks, heads, and figures rendered at several scales. The masks, some two dozen examples, are sheets of cast bronze with stereotyped features: straight mouths, aquiline noses, slanting almond-shaped eyes, broad brows, and prominent ears. By contrast, the fifty-seven heads are fully realized, with similar features set on cylindrical necks. Many of their skulls are flat on top, while a few are round; some have gold leaf applied to their faces. Plaited braids run down the back of their necks in some cases, while several variations on head gear are in evidence. The masks and heads, in turn, would seem to be quotations from a large standing figure. Fully 2.6 m tall with its base,

this figure stands in a frontal pose, two bare flat feet supporting a slim torso clothed in a robe with elaborate designs. Large arms raised at the shoulders end in oversized hands with sockets that cradled some object—perhaps an elephant tusk? The figure's head and a tall neck are completely comparable to the heads and masks. In this case a band is wrapped around the forehead and petals of a headdress rise above. A number of much smaller figures were also recovered, also with a general resemblance to this large example. It seems plausible therefore to link all of these objects to a ritual precinct or temple where they were displayed, perhaps as icons, effigies, or idols, or otherwise deco-

Bronze figure, Jinsha,
Chengdu (above)
Pit no. 2 during
excavation (right)

rated the site. The range of variation of their specific features suggests some differentiation of their identities as gods or ancestors, but their common traits suggest they are fundamentally a single population, whether human, superhuman, or otherwise. Since they were broken prior to burial in many cases, it has been suggested that they were stripped from a defunct edifice and ritually disposed.

Among many other enigmatic objects from these pits is a stand that stacks a ritual vessel (a square-section *zun*) atop four miniature figures on a base carried by a strange animal. The four figures again are much like the figure just discussed, although they wear only skirts. The vessel resting on their heads signifies a debt to the bronze casting of the middle Yangzi and North China regions, and indeed some *zun* vessels from the former were found in the two pits. But here the vessel is decorated with a hybrid ornament: more frontal figures across the central register, abstract decoration on the ring foot, and dimensional animals and birds at the shoulder. This is an iconography quite distinct from Shang cultures outside Sichuan, but one which suggests a debt to them by the appropriation of the *zun* vessel. A small kneeling figure bearing a simpler *zun* on its head was also found.

Boulders of several kinds of hard-stone have been found at the site, and may have been harvested in the Upper Yangzi region. Pits on the north side of the walled area could be evidence for working these stones at the site, and indeed the quantity of stone is a significant trait of the Sanxingdui pits. Very few objects, however, are actually true soft jade (nephrite). Many of the forms are blades and flat plaques (termed *zhang* scepters) that can only have had ceremonial

Bronze stand, pit no. 2

utility. Being thin and fragile, they were ill-suited to warfare or to use as tools. Scepters with a distinctive forked end (*yazhang*) are especially common, and their like have been documented over most of China Proper. These scepters were produced in an extremely elaborate array of types and variants. It may be that the Upper Yangzi was their origin during the late Neolithic and early Bronze Age.

Ancestors of Shu?

It is an accident of modern history that the archaeology of the Chinese Bronze Age began at Anyang (Ch. 4), now recognized as a ceremonial center and capital of the historic Shang kings. The state-level society of Anyang was the first literate culture of East Asia. It had many neighbors, more and less affected by interaction with the Great Settlement, and more and less known, in turn, to the Shang kings. In far distant Sichuan, beyond the Three Gorges and over the Qinling range, a contemporaneous society, which on present evidence was not literate, arose in one of the most fertile and resource-rich areas of all of China Proper.

Many scholars in Sichuan today claim this archaeological culture as Shu, an ancient people and kingdom of Sichuan known from historiographic tradition. But Shu, like many other peoples, cultures, or states known from ancient history cannot yet be documented back to the time of Sanxingdui. This identification, hopeful or optimistic now, sooner or later will be strengthened or weakened as additional work goes forward, especially at the sites around Chengdu. But whatever the name of the people at Sanxingdui might have been in the late second millennium BCE, they were surely not the Shang of North China. Another cultural tradition, distinct from those that arose in the North and Northwest (Xia, Shang, and Zhou), has been recovered. While other discoveries as rich as Sanxingdui have not yet been reported from the Yangzi drainage, it seems probably that cultures in those regions, also distinct from Shang and Zhou, will emerge ever more clearly over time. Finds in Hunan (especially large bells called *nao*) and in Jiangxi (the site at Wucheng and tomb at Xin'gan) may presage further developments.

Provincial museums throughout the south feature finds of the Shang and Zhou periods made in their areas. The Hunan Museum in Changsha and the Jiangxi Museum in Nanchang are especially well endowed in Bronze Age discoveries. The late Bronze Age Dian Culture of modern Yunnan is on display at the Yunnan Museum, Kunming. The archaeology of these and other "peripheral" regions has been enriched repeatedly by new discoveries. It may be best to think of Bronze Age China as a world of contemporary cultures as complex and varied as the Mediterranean and adjacent areas of Africa, Asia, and Europe.

SUGGESTED READING

The magnificent exhibition of material from Sanxingdui produced far and away the best source for all aspects of this remarkable site: *Ancient Sichuan: Treasures from a Lost Civilization,* ed. Robert Bagley (2001). Some of the same material is featured in Xiaoneng Yang, *The Golden Age of Chinese Archaeology* (1999). The culture is also introduced in the context of the Late Shang world in Robert L. Thorp, *China in the Early Bronze Age: Shang Civilization* (2005), pp. 249–63.

6 Zhou Yuan: Homeland of the Zhou

ZHOU YUAN MUSEUM
FUFENG, SHAANXI
WESTERN ZHOU PERIOD, C. 1046–771 BCE

For pre-modern Chinese scholars, study of antiquity began with the classics, a selection of texts placed at the center of the imperially sponsored curriculum for aspiring officials as early as the Han dynasty. These texts had been admired (and supposedly edited) by Confucius (b. 551 BCE). In his eyes and those of his followers, the classics portrayed an earlier world order that their own society could not match, a kind of Golden Age of sage rulers and ministers. After the campaigns at Anyang (Ch. 4) verified the historicity of the late Shang kings, attention naturally turned to ancient sites associated with the Western Zhou, the society portrayed in such classics as the *Book of Documents (Shu jing)* and *Book of Songs (Shi jing)*. But for most of the twentieth century, excavations at the Feng and Hao sites west of Xi'an and at sites around Luoyang were disappointing. Nothing for the early Zhou kings comparable to the palaces and royal tombs of the Shang could be found.

Work in the 1970s established the archaeological importance of an area straddling Fufeng and Qishan counties in Shaanxi, about 100 km west of Xi'an. Known as the Plain of Zhou (Zhou Yuan) in traditional sources, this region is located at the foot of Mount Qi, homeland of the Zhou people according to the *Book of Songs*. In fact, this area had been well known to late Qing scholars for important discoveries of bronze vessels, including many of the best-known Western Zhou inscriptions. Similar discoveries, over 100 by one count, continued from the 1950s into the 1970s. These finds documented the presence of elite Zhou lineages in this area early in the dynasty, as well as their apparent flight in the eighth century BCE (traditionally 771 BCE), with the Quan Rong incursion. Systematic excavations of the 1970s uncovered several clusters of well-preserved foundations in this same area, notably at Fengchu village (Qishan) and Zhaochen village (Fufeng).

Initially scholars debated the interpretation of these sites: Was the Fengchu compound datable before the conquest of Shang? Did a cache of thousands of oracle-bone fragments in a pit there actually reflect a Shang presence? Or were they Zhou divination

Grain offering vessel (hu gui)

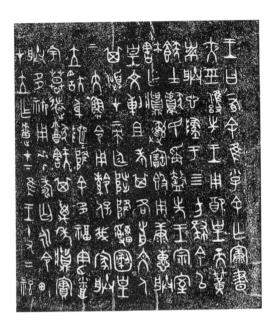

Rubbing of hu gui
inscription

records? The second, Zhaochen site, on the other hand, was clearly later, dating from the middle reigns of Western Zhou. If so, was this area the location of the ancestral temples of the Zhou kings? Would their tombs therefore be nearby? Recently (1999 to date) work has resumed at the Zhou Yuan sites under the auspices of the Institute of Archaeology (Beijing), the Shaanxi Institute of Archaeology (Xi'an), and Peking University. Near Yuntang village, between the earlier Fengchu and Zhaochen finds, two more compounds have been unearthed. These complexes correspond in their plans to ancestral temples as recorded in ritual canons, a better match in fact than earlier finds. Still more recently (2004), even more pregnant discoveries have been announced: more oracle-bones including some that name the Duke of Zhou, and large ramped tombs at a site named, significantly, the Duke of Zhou's Temple (Zhou Gong Miao). Perhaps the long search for the royal Zhou tombs is over.

During the mid-1970s, a succession of caches or hoards with bronze ritual vessels and bells were unearthed in the Zhou Yuan. Unlike burials, in which the chamber and furnishings can be reconstructed even when looting has taken place, a cache is generally bereft of clues like the pottery that allow dating. But the great asset of many of these caches has been lengthy inscriptions found on the vessels. The richest of these finds comprised 103 vessels and bells in a single pit near Zhuangbai village, Fufeng. The vessels were mostly inscribed, and their texts reveal many details of a family history. An inscription of 270 characters on a water basin tells of a scribe named Qiang and his descendants over four generations of service to the early Western Zhou kings. By rigorously cross-checking names and titles in these texts, scholars have reconstructed the descendants of Qiang, and in the process gleaned new data about the Zhou kings as well. These are primary sources, not unlike the oracle-bone inscriptions of the Shang kings found at Anyang. Most of these vessels are now in the collection of the Shaanxi History Museum, Xi'an.

The compound uncovered at Fengchu, the earliest of the several Zhou Yuan architectural sites now known, was also the best preserved. It anticipates the classic courtyard or quadrangle house (*sihe yuan*) of Beijing. Seen here in a rendering by Yang Hongxun of the Institute of Archaeology, Beijing, most of its details are carefully derived from physical evidence at the site. Even when only the base levels of a structure survive, it is possible to extrapolate the elevation and even the roof construction.

The Fengchu compound is a compact and self-contained unit built upon a raised platform of

At the Foot of Mount Qi

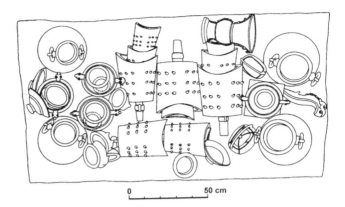

Zhuangbai cache

0   50 cm

pounded earth measuring 45 m north-south by 32m
east-west. It married an elevated hall, a large undivided
interior under a roof, with solid-walled chambers
more commonly found as workshops or dwellings.
The hall was placed just behind a median line dividing
the compound in half front and back. Its roof must
have joined or approached the roofed chambers on
each end; Yang shows these roofs intersecting. Steps or
ramps were required to ascend the hall, and its floor
was at the highest level within this compound. Yards in
front and rear were lower while the flanking rows of
chambers were elevated above them but below the hall
floor. From post holes dug into the foundation block,
a hall area of 17 m by 6 m with six intervals across and
three in depth can be inferred. The posts were carefully
aligned side-to-side, east to west, but not front to back.
Yang and others suggest this alignment accommodated
lateral tie-beams to rigidify the frame. True bays, however, were not created, since alignments in depth varied. Also unlike later bay systems, these posts were
anchored below floor level, rather than placed atop
stones on or above floor level. The hall was enclosed
on both ends and across the rear, but its south facade
was left open.

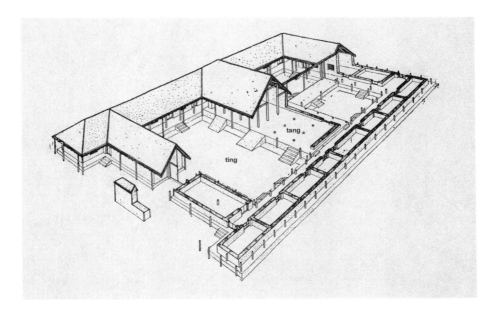

Rows of chambers on each long side and across the back enclosed the yards and main hall, with eight units on each side and five across the north. A maximum of twenty-one chambers might have been outfitted, in addition to two gate houses on the south. The walls of these chambers were constructed from pounded earth 60 to 90 cm thick, with some adobe and mud-plaster. Door and window openings likely faced the inside, allowing light to flow in from the yards. Roof overhang would have created a covered gallery fronting these chambers. This elevated walkway also allowed movement from front to rear off the central axis without crossing the main hall. All of the roofs in Yang's rendering are conjectural. However, the excavators found fragments of mud-plaster that retained impressions of beams and bundles of straw, possibly used between rafters. Meager quantities of broken roof tiles were also present at the site. Perhaps tiles were used only for covering ridges or as gutters

Fengchu compound rendering by Yang Hongxun

Peasants pounding earth,
Qian County

where slopes met. The Fengchu compound was entered from a central south gate. The yard within was a suitable assembly area for those invited to attend or participate in activities enacted in the raised hall.

Other architectural complexes now excavated at Zhou Yuan illustrate the evolution of both site plans and building techniques. The ensemble at Zhaochen, for example, shows a growing sophistication in foundations and frames. The columns of the main halls are supported by piers of stones piled in sockets (pits) within the pounded-earth foundation blocks. They were no longer set into post holes, as at Fengchu. The timber frame was also more regular, a step on the way to a true bay system. And the subdivision of the interior now defined both central spaces and end chambers. At the still later Yuntang and Qizhen sites, a new

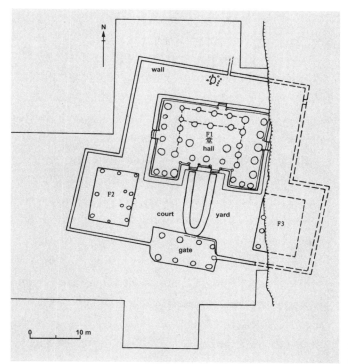

Plan of the Yuntang compound

site plan emerged, independent structures enclosing a courtyard within walls. The main hall interior featured a large open central bay, while flanking chambers extended forward at each end. More extensive use of pottery roof tiles was also much in evidence.

In the late second millennium BCE diverse populations inhabited the Wei River valley. The finds in Zhou Yuan are the best indicators for the location of the Zhou people on the eve of the conquest of Shang and for major lineages throughout the Western Zhou period. The Zhou Yuan architectural remains are better preserved than anything known to date from the Western Zhou capital sites, Feng and Hao near Xi'an, or at Anyang (Ch. 4). The Zhou population may have learned building technology from the Shang, but over

Western Zhou Archaeology

time they also carried it further. This process has parallels in both script and bronze casting. The Zhou Yuan oracle-bones utilize the same graphs created by the Shang, and Zhou bronze weapons and vessels follow norms established by foundries at Anyang. From these perspectives, the Zhou may have well been a distinct population, but they also shared a common culture with their neighbors the Shang to the east.

Outside the Wei River valley (Shaanxi), Western Zhou discoveries have been almost entirely rich cemetery sites. Important examples include the cemetery of the Dukes of Yan at Liulihe, Fangshan (outside Beijing, where there is also a walled site), the cemetery of the Dukes of Jin at Tianma-Qucun, Quwo (central Shanxi), and the cemetery of the Dukes of Guo at Sanmen (western Henan). Bronzes and jades from the Jin tombs are often displayed in Beijing at the Sackler Museum of Art and Archaeology, Peking University, which has led the excavations at Tianma-Qucun. The richness of intact graves at the latter two sites whets our appetites for news of the royal Zhou tombs in Zhou Yuan.

SUGGESTED READING

The most readable of the Zhou "classics" is *The Book of Songs*; see the translation by Arthur Waley (original 1937, many editions since). Western Zhou sites are treated by both Edward Shaughnessy and Jessica Rawson in *The Cambridge History of Ancient China* (1999). In spite of its date, prior to all of the archaeological evidence above, H.G. Creel's *The Origins of Statecraft in China: The Western Chou Empire* (1970) remains a fascinating read. Important bronzes from Zhou Yuan are featured in Xiaoneng Yang, *The Golden Age of Chinese Archaeology* (1999).

Suizhou: Marquis Yi's Chime

7

HUBEI PROVINCIAL MUSEUM
WUHAN, HUBEI
EASTERN ZHOU PERIOD, C. 433 BCE

Hubei is one of the largest provinces in China Proper, and for an archaeologist one of the richest in prehistoric and Bronze Age finds. The Hubei Provincial Museum, Wuhan, like other museums at the provincial level, has the mission of retelling the history of its region in line with the normative view of archaeology as history in the People's Republic. Yet the museum is devoted solely to the dramatic presentation of a single discovery from the fifth century BCE. And while Hubei was the heartland of the great state of Chu in this very period (Ch. 8), the find on display was actually the burial of an obscure local lord enfoeffed in a minor state called Zeng. From the standpoint of traditional sources—like the *Intrigues of the Warring States (Zhan guo ci)* or Sima Qian's *Records of the Grand Historian*—Marquis Yi, the marquis of Zeng, was in fact unknown. Why then devote an entire museum to his burial furnishings?

Marquis Yi was not totally obscure. Bronze bells catalogued in the Song dynasty (960–1279), the first great age for antiquarian study of ritual vessels, included ritual equipment made for a Marquis Yi of

Bell chime

Zeng by order of the King of Chu in the king's fifty-sixth year (433 BCE). While these objects were lost, this record has been well known to scholars. When a large and richly furnished tomb was opened north of Wuhan in Sui county (now Suizhou) in 1978, the Cultural Relics authorities immediately took note that 117 items carried inscriptions reading "made for the eternal use of Marquis Yi of Zeng." This tomb was replete with ten metric tons of bronze paraphernalia of every kind, including a chime of sixty-four musical bells. One bell still suspended from its frame, a type called *bo,* in fact carried the same inscription text known since the Song, affirming the attribution of this tomb to Marquis Yi and providing a date for the interment in the late fifth century BCE. At the time it was opened, the tomb at Suizhou was the first intact, large-scale, royal burial of the late Bronze Age to be properly excavated. It was, in short, our first glimpse into the highest level of late Zhou society, especially ritual and burial practices. No other province in China, to that date, could boast a discovery for the pre-Qin period even remotely comparable.

Chu territory in the fifth century BCE extended to the Dabie Mountains, a spur of the Qinling range that separates the North China Plain from the Yangzi drainage. This area, now in southern Henan and northern Hubei, was contested ground, occupied by a number of small principalities, which found themselves in the role of buffer states between Chu and its northern rivals. The kings of Chu alternately made alliances with and overpowered these polities. In the case of Zeng, which had a history extending to the Springs and Autumns period (8th to 5th centuries BCE), Chu made munificent gifts to solidify the allegiance of the rulers of Zeng, who had the rank of marquis (*hou*). According to the ritual norms of the Zhou, a local lord—a duke, marquis, earl, viscount, or baron—occupied the second tier of elite society, below the Son of Heaven, the king (*wang*) in Luoyang (Ch. 13), but above the ministers and great lords who served these rulers. But by the "Warring States" period (5th to 3rd centuries BCE), most powerful regional rulers had taken the title of king for themselves, and, as a result, their status possessions could usurp the prerogatives of the Son of Heaven. In the case of Marquis

An Underground Palace

Yi of Zeng, a vassal under the king of Chu, this meant
a set of sacrificial vessels as well as a huge musical
chime appropriate to a king. Thus the richness of this
tomb is compounded both by the generosity (self-
serving though it surely was) of the king of Chu, and
the violation of ritual and sumptuary standards that
gave a small, local ruler the status trappings of a Son of
Heaven.

In summer, 1977, construction workers from the
People's Liberation Army began to level a hilly plot
called Leigudun. They requested that local cultural
relics officials come to inspect the site, but this did not
happen until March, 1978. By that time, the hill had
been leveled and scrapped clean to reveal a layer of
large dressed stones that seemed to cap a huge excavation below. The work of probing, removing these
stones, and clearing the chambers below went forward
under the supervision of the provincial museum from
May 11th through June 28th. The excavation attracted
such crowds that much of the work was carried out
after dark. The tomb chamber was at a depth of 11 to

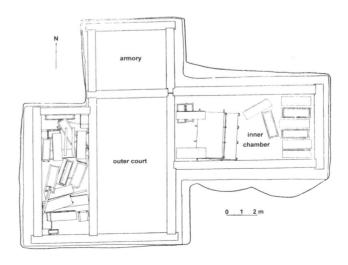

Plan of tomb chamber

13 m below ground level, set in sandstone bedrock, 21
m across and 16 m end to end (north-south). Charcoal
and sticky clay enveloped its huge catalpa timbers,
each about 50 cm square in section and 5 to 10 m in
length. When the largest timbers were removed, water-
logged, they weighed 1.5 tons. A large central chamber (almost 5 by 10 m) aligned north-south, held the
chime of bells and an array of ritual vessels placed
against the walls. The east chamber of similar dimensions housed the enormous double coffin of Marquis
Yi and nine much smaller coffins for eight females and
a dog. A square north chamber (4 by 4 m) served as an
armory, with hundreds of weapons, leather armor, and
chariot fittings. A west chamber (3 by 8.6 m) housed
thirteen additional small coffins, perhaps remains of
the court musicians. The chambers were filled with
water at the time excavation began, and a single rob-
ber's tunnel had punched into the central chamber
roof. Artifacts found in this area suggest that robbers
arrived on the scene in the late Warring States or Qin-
Han periods (3rd century), but they seem to have
taken little if anything from the tomb.

The Hubei Museum displays the contents of this
tomb by kind, and indeed the 15,000 items recovered
from the chambers in groups were grouped by function. The coffins are remarkable works of carpentry
and lacquer painting. Most are small boxes with
bulging sides and lids assembled using well-crafted
mortises and tenons. Marquis Yi's two coffins, however,
are another matter. The outer coffin is a large box constructed with a frame of bronze I-beams that hold
wooden panels. (Overall dimensions are 3.2 by 2.1 m
with a height of 2.2 m.) These panels were given lacquer-painted decoration; look for the small door

opening at the base of the foot end. Inside was the inner coffin, a rectangular box (2.5 m long and 1.3 m square) also replete with complex lacquer-painted designs. Here one sees not only panels like doors and windows but also a cohort of ten spear-carrying animal-like guardians on each side. The skeletal remains were those of a forty-five year old male. The twenty-one females in the smaller coffins ranged in age from fifteen to twenty-four. (The family hound was five to ten years old.)

The chime of musical bells remains the largest example of its kind known from ancient China. It was evidently made in a royal foundry of the kings of Chu, and bestowed on Marquis Yi in 433 BCE. The frame is L-shaped, in three tiers supported by small-scale bronze warrior figures. Two sets of twelve large bells with shanks are hung from the lowest level; the bell with the famous inscription was also placed there. The middle level carries three sets of thirty-three shank bells. The top levels carry three sets of nineteen loop-suspension bells. All of these bells were tuned, that is cast with such

Inner coffin decor

care and precision that they produce a pair of musical tones, depending on whether they are struck at the center or to the side of the lip. Thus sixty-four bells could create 128 tones. Moreover, detailed inscriptions on the bells designate the names of their notes in the musical scale of Chu and elaborate their relationship to scales used by other states. Scholars can use the tones produced by these bells to reveal the actual sounds of ancient Chinese music. (A smaller set of thirty-six bells was found in tomb no. 2 at Suizhou opened a few years later, but it is regarded as an inferior casting and came without either its stand or hardware.)

Bell chime figure

Mallets and striking poles, the implements used to play the bells, were also found. It is suggested that five musicians arrayed on two sides of the frame would have performed. Many other instruments filled out the court orchestra of Marquis Yi: a vertical drum, a chime of musical stones, several string instruments (zithers), and several wind instruments (pan pipes and flutes). The Hubei Musuem offers musical performances using reproduction instruments for visitors.

No less impressive are the complement of ritual vessels and weaponry deposited in the tomb. All but two of the 117 ritual vessels were found in the central chamber, which in symbolic function represented the court of the marquis. The tripods include nine in a characteristic Southern style with flaring loop handles at the rims, and a pair of massive cauldrons containing ox bones with long-handled serving ladles and lifting hooks. A set of eight covered serving vessels complement the nine tripods, as ritual norms dictated. Together they suggest a Dalao sacrifice appropriate to royal ritual. The most unusual vessels, however, are the unique pair of a wine container and a water basin, each covered with frothy interlaced three-dimensional dragons created by the lost wax technique rather than the ceramic piece-mold process. Two large wine containers, found in the armory, are the largest and heaviest vessels known from this period; they stand 1.26 m tall and weight around 300 kg each.

Tombs of Warring States Rulers

The discussion above by no means exhausts the varied contents of Marquis Yi's tomb. While hundreds of elite Zhou tombs from the fifth to third centuries have been excavated, none truly rivals the Suizhou burial for the combination of the rank of its master and the completeness of its furnishings. The examples discussed below, while impressive in their own right, inevitably highlight their own incomplete contents.

A contender in rank was King Cuo of the state of Zhongshan in Pingshan County, Hebei. His tomb, opened in 1974–78, was located in a funerary park outside the capital, Lingshou Cheng. The Zhongshan state, founded by the Bai Di, a steppe people, was brought under the control of the state of Wei in the early fourth century. It regained its relative independence thereafter and then allied with the northern powers Yan and Zhao, at which time it was known as a "thousand chariot state" in the parlance of the era. (Zeng was certainly much weaker militarily.) The tomb of King Cuo (c. 327–313?), the fifth Zhongshan ruler, was badly preserved. But treasuries located to the side of the main chamber were intact, and held an astonishing assortment of ritual gear, weapons, furnishings, and luxury objects like lamps and small-scale sculpture. In addition to these exceptional objects, the site retained the remains of an aboveground structure built around and atop the mound covering the burial.

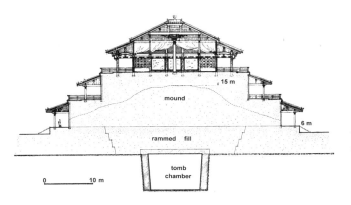

Mortuary temple,
Zhongshan site, Hebei

This was a sacrificial hall with galleries built into the flanks of its earthen core, part of a walled necropolis designed to hold five major burials and temples. The actual plan of this necropolis, cast in bronze, was also among the objects recovered.

Another example of a royal tomb, this one with structure intact, is the burial of a king of Yue at Yinshan outside Shaoxing, Zhejiang. This man-made earthen mound, one of five in a row, was disturbed in the 1990s and subsequently cleared by archaeologists in 1996 and 97. The mound was about 10 m high, with base dimensions of 72 by 36 m, and framed in turn by a moat that delimited the burial precinct. The wooden chamber within the mound was 33 m in length, 5 m wide at the base, and constructed as an A-frame. The king's coffin was a hollowed log 6 m in length. This tomb had been visited ten times by looters, who left behind a smattering a fine jades to suggest its original wealth of furnishings. It is tentatively ascribed to King Yunchang (r. 510–497), one of the last rulers of Yue before its extermination by the state of Wu. The combination of burial mound and moats sets this royal tomb apart from its peers, and strikes some observers as reminiscent of the mounded tombs of Japan, such as Nintoku's tumulus near Osaka.

The largest pre-imperial burial yet reported is from Fengxiang, Shaanxi, the site of the early Qin capital Yong. Tomb 1 opened in the 1980s was almost entirely empty, however, the handful of objects sad testimony to its attraction for dozens of looters over the centuries. The tomb measured 300 m end to end, with long ramps descending to a shaft with a depth of 24 m, its base dimensions 60 by 38 m. Large timbers were found at the center, their construction much like the chambers at Suizhou. This tomb is attributed to Duke Jing (r. 576–537). It is one of fourteen burial plots south of the Qin capital, each having one or more tombs without burial mounds.

These examples of Zhou-period royal tombs are among the most informative that survive from the pre-imperial era. They are dramatic evidence for the growth of regional powers, and for the widespread

Yinshan tomb, Shaoxing, Zhejiang

adoption of Zhou rites and social norms. One of the achievements of the First Emperor of Qin was to draw together these diverse plans in the design of his Lishan necropolis (Ch. 9).

Lothar von Falkenhausen, *Suspended Music: Chime-Bells in the Culture of Bronze Age China* (1993) is a wide-ranging account of every aspect of its topic. *Music in the Age of Confucius,* John Major and Jenny F. So, eds., (2000) is a catalogue of musical instruments from the period. Entries in Xiaoneng Yang, *The Golden Age of Chinese Archaeology* (1999) discuss many of the Suizhou ritual vessels and lacquer wares.

8 Jinan Cheng: The Great State of Chu

JINGZHOU MUSEUM
JINGZHOU-SHASHI, HUBEI
LATE ZHOU PERIOD, 5TH–3RD CENTURIES BCE

In the centuries before the creation of the empire, much of the territory of China Proper was dominated by seven strong states. These kingdoms claimed pedigrees from the Zhou kings of the late second millennium, but in this period they were only nominally loyal to the weakened royal Zhou court at Luoyang (Ch. 13). European scholars have compared this situation to feudalism breaking down. Over time, the orig-

Shaft of Baoshan tomb no. 2

inal bonds of blood and service dissolved as regional lords took royal prerogatives for themselves, and as large states swallowed weak ones.

The material cultures of these many states, at least at the level of their elites, were mixtures of Zhou customs and local elements. Ritual norms and burial practices might follow the prescriptions of Zhou ritual, while music and dance, decorative art and dress exhibited distinctive styles. The states of the center—Han, Wei, and Zhao, descendants of the great state of Jin—were, like royal Zhou, self-proclaimed Hua-Xia people of the "central plains" (*zhong yuan*). They saw their neighbors to the north and south as "others." States of the North and Northwest—Yan, Qin, and the smaller Zhongshan—all interacted with steppe peoples. The customs of Wu and Yue, to the southeast (the lower Yangzi), and of Ba and Shu, to the southwest (the Upper Yangzi), were frequently remarked upon as strange, even exotic by writers from the central plains. The two most powerful of the "seven strong states" were Qi, on the Shandong peninsula, and Chu, its territory straddled the Middle Yangzi drainage of modern Hubei and Hunan. The three great rivals at the end of this period—Qin, the ultimate victor, Chu, and Qi, the last to surrender—could well have seen their fates reversed. Chu or Qi might plausibly have won final victory and perhaps created its own version of the first imperial state. Had either done so, later history would surely have been much different.

A Bronze Age Capital

In recent times a myriad construction projects and salvage excavations in Henan, Hubei, and Hunan have unearthed the material legacy of the powerful state of Chu. The capital of Chu was north of the Yangzi River

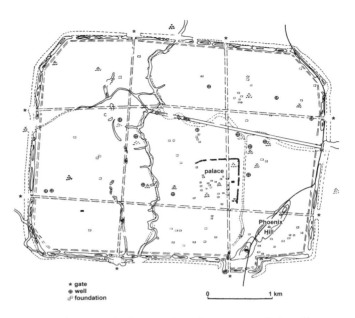

Plan of Jinan Cheng

★ gate
⊕ well
⊡ foundation

0 _____ 1 km

in modern Hubei, a region known traditionally as Jingzhou. This capital, called Ying, is the walled site at Jinan Cheng, less than 10 km north of the great river amid low hills, lakes, and marshes. The modern city of Jing-Sha, the consolidation of the two river towns Jiangling and Shashi, is now a stop for boats moving up and down the river to or from the Three Gorges. The Jingzhou Museum inside the well-preserved Ming walls of old Jiangling draws its collections from the surrounding region once dominated by the ancient Chu capital.

The city walls of Ying were probably built in the early fifth century during the reign of King Hui (488–432). They extend some 3.5 km north–south and 4.5 km east–west, enclosing more than three times the area of Ming Jiangling. The walls of Ying are a major feature on the landscape, with base dimensions 30 to 40 m across and heights of 4 to 7 m. Made of pounded earth, they are encircled in turn by a wide moat of 50 to 60 m set out from the walls another 20 to 40 m. Again the contrasts in scale with the smaller Ming wall and moat are striking. Gates breached the walls of Ying for access both by water and land. Water gates on north and south, and two land gates on each of the four sides have been surveyed. Several large water channels run across the city, as did several major roads connecting opposite gates. More than 300 foundations have been identified within these walls, at least eighty dated to the late Zhou-period Chu occupation. Half that number are concentrated in a walled area southeast of the city center, probably the royal palace. Water wells are ubiquitous throughout the site; hundreds have been examined for their contents.

However, the richest veins for the culture of Chu are extensive cemeteries in virtually every direction outside the walls. In these tracts, some 800 large mounded tombs have been counted, of which forty have been excavated to date. Two sites extending east from the capital walls—Yutai Shan and Jiudian—yielded tombs spanning the late Springs and Autumns period through the late Warring States period (c. 6th to 3rd centuries BCE). The Yutai Shan excavations, between November, 1975 and January, 1976, followed a strip of land 1050 m long and 80 m wide to clear 554 tombs. The Jiudian campaigns, which stretched over a decade from the late 1970s to the late 1980s, opened 597 tombs. Although many of these burials had been damaged, either by looters or natural causes, their immense quantities of tomb chambers and furnishings constitute the richest body of material of this kind for any part of China in the late Bronze Age.

The richest Chu tombs, however, were considerable distances from the city, set apart from cemeteries like those mentioned above. The Tianxingguan tombs, for example, were 25 km east, overlooking Chang Lake. The Baoshan tombs were 16 km north of the city, and many other sizeable burials have been cleared in hills north and west of the walls. The largest of these Jiangling area burials exemplify the funerary practices of the Chu nobility. While it is unlikely any reported so far are actually royal interments (see Ch. 7, the Suizhou tomb), they are remarkable achievements nonetheless. Their most noteworthy contents fill the galleries of the Jingzhou Museum.

Major tombs have large burial mounds surmounting deep vertical shafts. Tianxingguan tomb no. 1, the largest yet reported, was covered by an earthen mound 70 m in diameter and 7 m in height. The mound of Baoshan tomb no. 2 was somewhat smaller, at 54 m in diameter and 5.5 m in height. The shaft of the former tomb measured 41 by 37 m at ground level and the latter 34 by 32 m. In each case a series of steps, fifteen or fourteen respectively, reduced the shaft dimensions, leaving an area for the burial chambers of 8.2 by 7.5 m or 6 by 6 m, respectively. (These steps may have been used by mourners at the time of the funeral.) Such tomb chambers required huge quantities of wood, 182 timbers for Baoshan tomb no. 2 alone. The chambers were rectangular structures consisting of a central coffin area and outer compartments for furnishings. In each, a three-layer coffin held the mortal remains. Two thousand or more grave goods were taken from surrounding compartments by the excavators.

The superior design and construction of these coffins and chambers protected the perishable grave goods in these and other burials around Jiangling. A coat of sticky clay usually enveloped the outer chamber, sometimes with a fill of charcoal (Ch. 12, Mawangdui). Timbers were tightly joined; for coffins, lids and bodies were tied with silk bindings and sealed tight with lacquer. In both north and south, an assortment of bronze ritual vessels, weapons, and chariot fittings are the expected contents of elite burials, and Chu tombs have something of all the above. What the Jiangling tombs add is a variety of wooden objects, usually lacquered, from musical instruments (drums and zithers) to carvings of figurines and apotropaic guardians. Basketry and textiles also survive in quantity. A humble grave at Mashan, northwest of the Chu capital—a single coffin in a small chamber—held thirteen layers of silk shrouds and twenty silk garments including a hat and three pairs of slippers. Wooden and bamboo slips used for writing documents have also been preserved in many Chu burials, over 400 from Baoshan tomb no. 2, for example. Lacquer wares and textiles are displayed in special galleries at the Jingzhou Museum.

The customs of the Chu elite merged Zhou ritual and local cultural style. The interlace designs embroidered onto silk textiles and garments have their counterparts in lacquer painting and in wood carvings. A small arm rest is composed of birds, serpents, and other creatures artfully juxtaposed. A drum stand has a base of addorsed felines and long-necked birds. Fearsome creatures with long tongues that guard tomb chambers chomp on serpents and carry a rack of deer antlers. This pictorial content would seem to correspond to the exotic imagery of poetry from southern regions collected in *The Songs of the South* (*Chu ci*) and of fantastic texts like the *Classic of Mounains and Seas* (*Shan hai jing*).

The customs and style of Chu survived into the Han period, and account for one of the feature attrac-

Embroidery from
Mashan tomb no. 1

tions of the Jingzhou Museum. Han tomb no. 168 at
Phoenix Hall (Fenghuangshan), a low ridge inside the
city walls of Ying, was opened in 1975. By the standards of the pre-imperial Chu nobility, this was a
minor grave. It was not damaged after interment,
however, and held the well-preserved corpse of a
sixty-year-old male, named Sui according to his personal seal. Mr. Sui was a low-ranking local official of
the Han imperial government, and so entitled to few
grave goods. His tomb held personal items like a stiff
gauze hat, hemp slippers, a writing kit (brush, knife,
and ink), as well as a complement of wooden attendant figurines, a few ceramics, and a selection of lacquer wares. A document written on a wooden slip

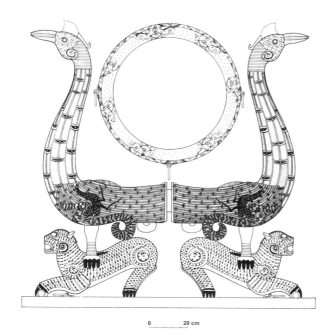

0   20 cm

Drum stand
from Tianxingguan
tomb no. 2

announced Sui's imminent funeral to the Lord of the Burials, an official who apparently supervised the underworld. Thus this local official's personal attendants interacted with a parallel bureaucracy of the underworld. This slip provides a rare glimpse into concepts of the afterlife and underworld in early Han times. The date of this document and the burial is 167 BCE.

The superior construction of Chu burials has preserved objects of kinds that must have existed in elite society in the other Warring States. Unfortunately, in most provincial and regional museums it is perdurable objects that are displayed: fired clay, bronze and iron, and stone. Thus while courts such as Qi (modern Shandong) or Qin (Shaanxi) must have had their own courtiers attired in fine silks eating from lacquer dishes and cups, those kinds of objects are rarely encountered

Warring States Capitals

outside the realm of Chu. Thus evidence from the material culture of Chu in many cases represents the broader culture of the period.

Other regional cultures of the late Zhou period are less often encountered by travelers. Still, all of the major capitals have been enrolled on the national and provincial registers: notably, Linzi (state of Qi; Linzi, Shandong), Xiadu (state of Yan; Yixian, Hebei), Yong (state of Qin; Fengxiang, Shaanxi), and Handan (state of Zhao; Handan, Hebei). Pre-imperial Qin objects are showcased upon occasion at the Museum of Terra Cotta Warriors and Horses and the Shaanxi History Museum, Xi'an. The pre-imperial Qin capital near modern Fengxiang has been extensively investigated; some of that material is also at Baoji. The archaeology of Qi is on display both at the Shandong Provincial Museum in Ji'nan and at the capital site near modern Linzi. Enormous chariot pits here are a staggering sight. The Henan Provincial Museum, Zhengzhou, has a selection of Eastern Zhou materials on display from several late Zhou states, including Zheng and Chu.

SUGGESTED READING
A general treatment of the later Bronze Age is found in *The Cambridge History of Ancient China* (1999) in chapters by Mark Edward Lewis and Wu Hung. Xiaoneng Yang, *The Golden Age of Chinese Archaeology* (1999), treats a selection of media, some from the Jingzhou Museum. Constance Cook and John Major, eds., *Defining Chu: Image and Reality in Ancient China* (1999) offer a collection of essays on many aspects of this culture, its history, archaeology, and art. David Hawkes' translation of *The Songs of the South* (1985) and Anne Birrell's edition of *The Classic of Mountains and Seas* (1999) are both recommended.

Qin and Han

(221 BCE–220 CE)

The final military success of the Qin armies in 221 BCE was a watershed in Chinese history, as well as a firm historical date that defines the beginnings of Imperial China. China remained an imperial state until 1912, although some observers see signs of an imperial mentality even in the present day.

The man who usually gains credit for this momentous achievement was Ying Zheng, the Duke of Qin (r. 246–210 BCE). By his time, the Qin state had already expanded in several directions from its base in the northwest, modern Shaanxi and Gansu, notably to the south, where it took over the Upper Yangzi region of Sichuan in the fourth century. Under a minister known as Lord Shang (350s BCE), the Qin state had also created a tightly-regulated population, state-dominated economy, and a powerful, disciplined army. After Ying Zheng's accession at age 13, he and his advisors began further expansion. In the decade following 230 BCE, Qin armies took the field and systematically overran the powerful eastern states. In 221, with the demise of Qi, the young Duke took a new title, First August Sovereign (*shi huang di*), to proclaim his new status and the new system he ruled. An area that had once been seven large states (Ch. 8) was now a single regime, controlled from Xianyang (near modern Xi'an). This empire was administered as thirty-six commanderies, each with a civil governor, military commander, and censor appointed by the court and responsible directly to it. Weapons throughout the empire were confiscated and melted; defensive walls between the former states and around their cities were torn down. Unified weights and measures were imposed, as was a standard script. Old walls along the northern frontier were connected and improved, the beginnings of the Great Wall, and rapid roadways were built like spokes radiating from the capital to improve communications. From our perspective, however, the most conspicuous legacy of the First Emperor is his tomb complex (Ch. 9, Lishan).

Imperial Qin did not long outlive the First Emperor himself (d. 210 BCE). The new regime that replaced it, the Han, founded by the commoner Liu Bang, retained so many Qin institutions and policies, however, that Qin's legacy was not lost. Han accounts of the First Emperor vilify the man, but in fact most of Han imperial administration and many of its economic, legal, and social policies perpetuated Qin models. This emulation extended also to the Han imperial tombs (Ch. 10, Yangling). And the Han, in spite of a hiccup in the early first century CE, endured for over four centuries. Even as China descended into a period of disunion, Han remained a model of the way "all under Heaven" ought to be. Indeed the Sui and Tang overtly sought to recreate the Han imperium.

The history of Qin and Han is preserved in four early texts: the *Records of the Grand Historian* of Sima Qian, the two Han histories (early and late, or Western and Eastern), and a history of the three states that divided the map in the third century CE. These texts were the models for later court-commissioned histories, and provide a wealth of detail, especially in their monographs and biographies. Han archaeology has been exceptionally rich and diverse. Han sites are widespread, from the far northeast (modern Korea) to the extreme southwest (Yunnan and Vietnam), and extending northwest up the Gansu corridor (Ch. 20, Mogao).

In retrospect, the unification by the Qin and the perpetuation of the imperial system by Han mark the creation of "China." (Indeed, our name "China" may derive from "Qin.") Prior to 221 BCE, the map of North and Central China was divided in every way; after that date an imposed unity began that has continued, in spite of interruptions, to modern times. Regions with their own cultures and customs were subsumed within a larger entity that insisted on common interests and identities. While many regional customs (like speech) have survived over the last two thousand years, both the veneer and the realities of a shared cultural identity have tended to subordinate them, especially in the eyes of foreigners who came to China only late in its history.

The standard account of this period is D. Twitchett and M. Loewe, eds., *The Cambridge History of China,* vol. 1, *The Ch'in and Han Empires, 221 B.C.–A.D. 220* (1986). Burton Watson's translation of *Shi Ji* makes good reading; see *Records of the Grand Historian of China,* 2 vols. (1961 and later editions).

SUGGESTED READING

9 Lishan: The First Emperor's Army

MUSEUM OF QIN WARRIORS AND HORSES
LINTONG, EAST OF XI'AN, SHAANXI
QIN, 221–206 BCE
WORLD HERITAGE SITE

Since their discovery in 1974, the underground warriors of the Qin First Emperor have generated excitement around the world, more so than any other development in Chinese archaeology over the last fifty years. They epitomize many of the things we expect from archaeology: an unexpected and compelling glimpse into the past, fascinating historical context, stunning scale and quality. In Chinese history, the warriors and their tomb setting are material evidence for the advances that created the first empire and with it "China." Familiar by now through media and exhibitions, the warriors nonetheless never fail to take away the breath of visitors as they view the trenches for the first time.

Terra Cotta Warriors

The discovery and subsequent investigation of the underground army are models for how archaeology and cultural relics policy are intended to work in the People's Republic. In March, 1974, farmers digging a well found large pieces of baked clay (terra cotta) several meters below the village orchard they were working in. They reported their find to local authorities

who in turn called in experts from Xi'an, the provincial capital. The pieces of clay were fragments of large human figures—heads, shoulders, arms—and reminiscent of several kneeling figurines previously recovered near the outer wall of the tomb of the First Emperor of Qin (d. 210 BCE), an historic site placed on the national register by the State Council in 1961. But this well was 1200 m east of that wall, and seemed to promise quantities of broken figures far greater than the solitary kneeling examples. With permission and budgetary support from the National Cultural Relics Bureau, an excavation 60 m across and 15 m wide was begun, revealing hundreds of shattered figures. The figures had been installed in a gallery running north-south and corridors aligned east-west; the excavation was clearly only part of a larger site awaiting investigation. The archaeologists started probing that soon revealed a trench over 210 m long east-west and about 70 m across north-south. This trench (no. 1) was

Lishan mound

divided into nine corridors by baulks of earth, with narrower flanking corridors on both long sides and galleries at each end. Based on initial sampling, archaeologists estimated the trench held about 6000 life-size terra cotta warriors with several chariot teams and quantities of bronze weaponry. The State Council then authorized construction of a site museum, a hangar-like structure without internal supports, which opened to the public on October 1, 1979.

Cultural Relics policies were no less essential to subsequent investigations at the site. In probing the margins of trench no. 1 prior to construction of the hangar, two additional trenches were located on its north. Trench no. 2 at the east end was a more complicated structure with a mix of ninety chariots and 1400 figures including cavalry and striding and kneeling archers. Trench no. 3 near the west end, a much smaller pit, held an assortment of figures that may represent a command unit. After construction over Trench no. 1 was completed, it was possible to excavate and enclose these two trenches with their own structures as well. These two trenches have since opened to the public, but excavations inside trench no. 2 are still in progress.

Plan of initial excavation, 1974–75

Meanwhile more work was accomplished in the immediate area of the emperor's tomb. Survey and

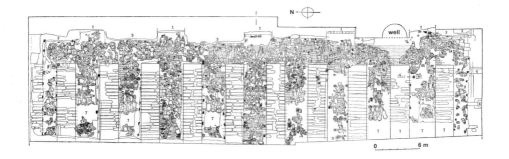

N

well

0   6 m

probing throughout the 1980s and 90s created a steady procession of new finds inside and outside the outer and inner walls of the necropolis. The most remarkable was a small trench opened in 1980 with several wooden compartments once covered by the skirt of the mound. In one part of this structure, two bronze chariots something less than half life-size were found, albeit crushed into hundreds of pieces. Restoration of these two chariots took most of that decade. Both are now displayed in the lower level of the museum at the north side of the plaza in front of trench nos. 1 through 3.

The apparent megalomania of the First Emperor is a strong element of both historical and popular accounts. Later scholars castigated Ying Zheng for the grand scale of his capital, with hundreds of palaces on both sides of the Wei River connected by screened roadways and bridges so that no one would know where the sovereign was spending the night. When the capital fell to the rebel army of Xiang Yu, its structures burned for months. These palaces and the tomb, known as Lishan after the nearby mountains, were constructed over a decade by a labor force reported to number 700,000, ostensibly one-eighth of the population. The cruelty of the Qin regime—the emperor, his ministers, and draconian laws—was exemplified by the sufferings of these laborers as well as those impressed to remake the long walls that defined the frontier with steppe peoples across the north. Other alleged misdeeds, such as the burning of the books or burying Confucian scholars alive, became part of a litany of the "Faults of Qin," factors that historians argued led to its rapid demise upon the First Emperor's death.

Bronze chariot

Some of what popular legend says may be grounded in fact. But in hindsight, the tomb serves as an analogy for the practices required to create a unified, imperial state, the first in East Asian history. That state, like the tomb project, required careful planning, the ability to muster human resources (army, bureaucrats, labor) and to requisition natural resources (clay, wood, stone, metal). Both enterprises would fail if the ability to control men and materials fell behind schedule or missed targets. While harsh laws and cruelty may indeed have been a part of that mix, so too were the practical necessities to house, clothe, and feed laborers or soldiers, the ability to integrate the efforts of planners, master artisans, and unskilled workers, and the capacity to monitor quality and insure the success of each task. If these phrases anticipate the vocabulary of modern state institutions, that is no accident. To create the terra cotta army as part of a much larger, more complex necropolis is an impressive demonstration of the capacities of the new, imperial institution.

Visitors to the Museum of Warriors and Horses pass the tomb site on the highway coming from Xi'an, but it is not often visited. The area around the necropolis has been extensively investigated since the 1980s, and has revealed a staggering number of features that would surprise anyone walking the site. The mound as seen from the road is a slumping four-sided pyramid covered with green bushes, the pomegranates for which the area is known, and surrounded by fields of winter wheat. This man-made cenotaph was erected after the interment of the First Emperor deep underground in a vertical shaft that so far has only been probed. We know the square shaft is framed below ground level by an earthen wall about 4m wide and tall, and that the shaft may reach a depth of 30m. Multiple openings in the wall, five on the east in particular, allow access to chambers at the base of the shaft, but they cannot yet be described. A structure combining dressed stone and huge timbers would be likely. Geological prospecting in the mid-1980s reported extraordinarily high concentrations of ambient mercury in the area of the shaft under the mound. This finding may support Sima Qian's account of mercury representing seas and rivers circulated through a topographical map of the world on the floor of the burial chamber.

While no other trenches with hundreds or thousands of warriors have been found outside the necropolis since the 1970s, the number of sites, features, pits, and burials now located numbers in the thousands. At least 180 pits have been identified in the precinct around the mound and walls, including the bronze chariots. Among recent discoveries from 1998 and 1999 are stone helmets and body armor for both warriors and horses; life-size terra cotta figures representing a company of acrobats, stout strong men who manipulated a large bronze tripod, found with them, as a part of their act; and a cohort of high-ranking officials. Yet another trench opened in 2000 almost a kilometer northeast of the outer wall held bronze water fowl—swans, geese, and cranes—around a water course perhaps intended to evoke the imperial menagerie. Such finds have been featured in the lobby of the museum in recent years. Still other discoveries include skeletal remains of exotic animals, horse burials with kneeling attendants, modest tombs that may

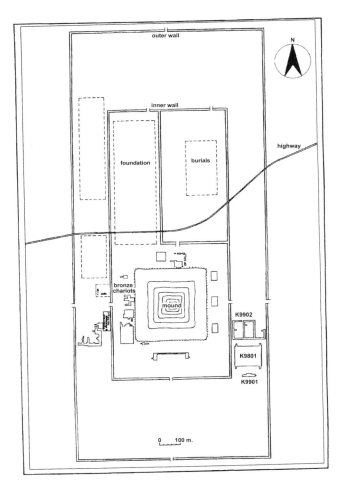

Plan of Lishan necropolis

belong to members of the imperial family or inner court officers, and, at some remove, cemeteries for the laborers who created the necropolis as well as kilns and a stone workshop. As these myriad finds accumulate, it becomes clear that the designers of the tomb complex were intent on incorporating all facets of the life style of the First Emperor, validating his unique status in society and in history. By drawing together strands from mortuary traditions of previous centuries and other states, they created a model for later imperial burials, as we will see in the Han and Tang imperial tombs (Ch. 10 and Ch. 18) west of Xi'an.

Remains of the First Emperor's capital lie north and west of Xi'an. The Xianyang Palaces on terraces north of the Wei River were excavated in the 1970s. While there is little now to see, the view overlooking the river valley is impressive. The Afang (or Ebang) Palace, west of Xi'an, has recently been investigated. Its front hall foundation measured 1270 m east-west by 426 m north-south; its height is as much as 12 m. This massive mound of hard-pounded earth was designed to carry the main audience hall of the First Emperor, but apparently never completed. The pre-imperial Dukes of Qin occupied a capital (Yong) near modern-day Fengxiang well west of Xi'an (see Ch. 8); its walls and some structures have been reported. The large royal cemetery stretches south of the ancient city, and yielded the largest tomb ever opened (fully 300 m from end to end) in the 1980s. Unfortunately it was almost totally looted; a handful of finds are displayed in the Shaanxi History Museum, Xi'an.

Qin Archaeology

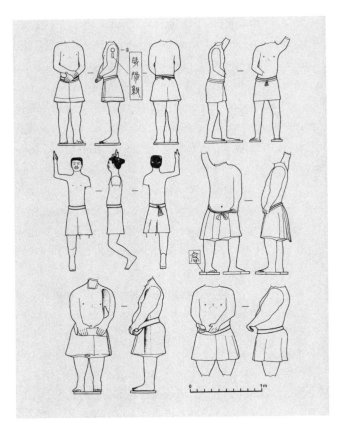

Acrobats, trench K9901

SUGGESTED READING   The best historical treatment of Qin in English is Derk Bodde's chapter in *The Cambridge History of China,* vol. 1, *The Ch'in and Han Empires, 221 B.C.–A.D. 220* (1986). Two useful introductions to the terra cotta warriors are Maxwell Hearn, in Fong, *The Great Bronze Age of China* (1980), and Ladislav Kesner, in Yang, *The Golden Age of Chinese Archaeology* (1999). Burton Watson's translation of the annals of the First Emperor mixes credible history and exaggeration; see *Records of the Grand Historian: Qin Dynasty* (1993); Jia Yi's classic essay on the "Faults of Qin" comprises pp. 74-83.

Yangling: The Han Imperial Tombs

10

HAN YANGLING MUSEUM
XIANYANG, NORTHWEST OF XI'AN, SHAANXI
WESTERN HAN PERIOD, C. 141–126 BCE

Driving along the highway from the airport to Xi'an, visitors begin to experience the "Land within the Passes" (*guan zhong*). This terrain is draped in thick deposits of loess, fine, yellow-brown soil that has blown into the Wei River valley since the last Ice Age. The road follows an elevated terrace south of the mountains on the north but well above the flood plain. Only occasionally does a distant view of the river or the Qinling Mountains beyond come into view. Just before the highway descends to the new Wei River bridge, two enormous earthen mounds loom on the north, the twin burials of the Han emperor Jing (Liu Qi, r. 156–141 BCE) and his empress née Wang (d. 126 BCE). This is Yangling, the eastern-most of nine Western Han imperial necropolises stretching westward almost 40 km from Han Chang'an. And because of this highway, the Yangling is now the best known of any Han imperial burial.

A Han Necropolis

In May 1990, probing along the path of this new highway reached the Yangling. Using a device called a Luoyang spade—originally the tool of grave robbers

Armored figurines, trench no. 20, Yangling

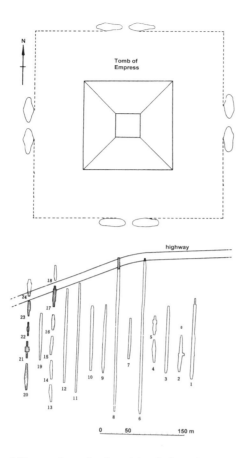

Plan of southern trenches

(see p. 10)—archaeologists hired for this task came
upon trenches deep underground south of the mound
of the Empress Wang. These trenches occupied an area
more than 300 m square; the twenty-four separate pits
were aligned in fourteen parallel north–south rows
spaced at 20 m intervals. The trenches reached depths
7 to 8 m below ground, and ranged from 25 m to as
much as 291 m in length. Although the wooden
chambers had long ago decayed, their contents were
intact: ceramic figurines as well as an assortment of
other objects. The excavators were startled to find that
the human figurines lacked clothing and arms, rare
examples of nudity in early Chinese art.

Two of the longest trenches, K6 and K8, were cleared first because they lay across the route of the new highway. Although they had been looted, one area of 80 sq m still had over 500 figurines in place. Another trench also affected by the road, K17, was entirely cleared in 1990 and 1991; it revealed miniature wooden chariots and earthenware horses as well as more figurines and bronze grain measures. Four more trenches, K20 through K23, were also cleared in 1991, exposing more of the same, but also livestock: oxen, rams, sheep, pigs, dogs, and chickens. Many of the human figurines from these trenches had remnants of armor still affixed to their torsos as well as miniature bronze and iron arrows and lances. By 1999, all or part of fourteen trenches had been investigated, and a museum display opened nearby.

The most obvious significance of the Yangling finds lies in their reprise of the First Emperor's tomb (Ch. 9). Like the Lishan necropolis, the Yangling complex represents the status and life style of the imperial person, the Son of Heaven. So military formations, fully equipped, as well as the resources to sustain them (grain, livestock, and weaponry) were provided. At the same time, at Yangling, these were miniature figurines (about 60 cm tall) and animals. The weapons they carry were also miniaturized, not the contents of a real arsenal as in the trenches at Lishan. Symbolic and status agendas were honored at Yangling, but realized in a more modest, economical fashion. Nonetheless, this more pragmatic approach required figurines dressed in suits of armor, with movable arms (now missing) to manipulate tiny swords and lances.

Liu Qi, posthumously called Jing Di, the fourth Han sovereign, presided over a period of economic growth. He faced a serious challenge in 154 BCE when imperial princes, enfoeffed in the east, revolted. Suppressing them consolidated the power of the imperial capital, and Han princes were never again a serious threat to the emperors. (Their tombs are prominent in Han archaeology, however; see Ch. 11.) Liu Qi also had to buy peace from his steppe neighbors, the Xiongnu (Huns). His son Liu Che (Wu Di) finally resolved that problem by military force.

The finds of 1990 led to investigation of the entire site, making it today the best documented Han imperial tomb. Well east of the twin mounds lay a walled town called Yangling Yi, whose population provided the tax revenue to keep up the imperial necropolis. Prosperous in its day, it was home to a number of capital luminaries. Approaching from the east was the processional path, with burials laid out both north and south of the roadway. These tracts rewarded faithful relatives and officials associated with Jing Di; they extend over 3.5 sq km. About one hundred family plots have been surveyed, and over thirty small mounds recorded. The tomb precinct of the emperor stands at the west end of this path, flanked by that of the empress to the northeast. Each tomb is enclosed by a square wall; the emperor's is over 400 m on a side, the wall itself 3 m thick. Gates on each side with passages 12 to 14 m wide controlled access; their thick

Section of trench no. 20

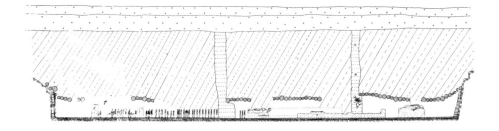

foundation blocks are still prominent on the surface. Jing Di's burial mound is about 170 m square and rises to a height of 32 m. Each of these components is scaled slightly smaller for Empress Wang.

The trenches located near the highway are merely a fraction of a much larger array. The southern zone is balanced by a northern zone of fourteen more rows northwest of the emperor's precinct. Within the emperor's walled area, moreover, eighty more trenches have been located. They come in different sizes, but were aligned perpendicular to the skirt of the mound on all four sides. South of the emperor's walled mound are two large architectural complexes, probably ritual sites where sacrifices to the deceased could be performed. The archaeological site museum lies south of the empress's mound and trenches. To avoid all of this, the new highway weaves its way westward between trenches, walls, and gates. Well to the rear (west) of the entire site is a plot of convict burials, the men who died with their shackles on while performing the hard labor of building the necropolis.

The Wider Context: Han Tombs

Eleven Western Han sovereigns were interred near the Han capital, Chang'an; nine of their tombs are sited on the terraces above the Wei River. The largest of these establishments was created for Jing Di's heir, Liu Che, known to history as Wu Di (r. 140–87 BCE), the "martial emperor." His precinct, the Maoling, is surrounded by a wall 430 m square; his mound is 230 m on each side (as compared to Jing Di's 170 m) and rises to 46m in height (compared to 32 m). Whereas Jing Di had a dozen years to construct his tomb (c. 153–141), Wu Di enjoyed the longest reign of Western Han, with fifty-three years to devote to his eternal resting place. A tradition recorded in the *History of the Jin* (compiled in the seventh century) claims that Maoling was looted by thousands of rebels at the end of Western Han, but "they could not reduce by half the contents of the tomb." Excavation of a trench located southeast of Maoling and associated with Wu Di's elder sister, the Yangxin Princess, revealed such treasures as a gilt bronze censer and gilt horse that today are among the treasures of the Shaanxi History Museum. Also near Maoling, a jade animal-mask escutcheon 30 cm square was retrieved from a ditch in the 1970s. If the escutcheon held a functional door pull, as it should, one then must picture a luxurious building outfitted with jade hardware!

The contents of Maoling and Yangling range from precious materials to earthenware architectural pottery and figurines. Such goods were the responsibility of the Artisan of the Eastern Garden, a court workshop that manufactured the necessary accessories of an imperial burial, as well as some required by the Han princes established in their outlying fiefs. With the Court Architect and military, corvée, and convict laborers, the craftsmen of the Eastern Garden workshop made the material legacy we encounter today at the imperial tombs. Kilns that produced figurines in large quantities are among recent discoveries in the northwest corner of Han Chang'an. So far, twenty-seven kilns have been unearthed near the site of the city's Western Market. The largest of these kilns could accommodate 450 figurines of the kind found near Yangling, stacked upside down in rows with their heads in the sand floor of the firing chamber. The products of these kilns were sent to the Yangling, but also to at least three other imperial burials (Maoling, Pingling, and Duling).

Warrior figurines,
Yangjiawan

If the Yangling figurines were not strictly nudes (by definition a conscious display of the human body), they were nonetheless high quality grave furnishings. Their manufacture was part of a transition from the life-size scale of the Lishan necropolis to the reduced scale customary from Han onwards. Clay human figurines of exceedingly crude form are documented in some pre-Qin burials, especially in Shandong (the state of Qi), while a tradition of carved wooden figurines flourished in parts of the south (the state of Chu). However, both types seem almost irrelevant as models for the First Emperor's army. But the Qin model was definitely in the minds of the artisans assigned to furnish the Western Han imperial tombs. The Han figurines were fashioned in two-part molds; front and back halves impressed bodily forms in slabs of soft clay. At the beginning of Western Han, clothing

was modeled as a part of the body. The best known examples are from Yangjiawan, a site near the Changling of the Han founder, Liu Bang. (Reproductions of these figurines are displayed at the Yangling site museum; the real items are at the Shaanxi History Museum and Xianyang City Museum.) After firing, their clothing and faces were painted. The more naturalistic Yangling figurines had their heads fashioned separately. For reasons unknown, many more heads survive in the trenches and at the kilns than do bodies. Both heads and bodies were made in a limited number of types, but could be stamped out in quantity. Cavalry riders with wide-spread legs sit astride their horses. By contrast, their predecessors from Yangjiawan had torsos affixed to the horse, the legs modeled as a part of the animal. At the Yangling, there were model animals as well. This tradition of tomb

Stone horse, tomb of Huo Qubing, Maoling

furnishings—figurines, animals, even architectural models—continued through late imperial times, including even some Ming tombs. Its artistic high point is the Tang (Ch. 18, Zhaoling and Qianling).

The Shaanxi History Museum has a wide selection of tomb figurines from Qin and Han sites in the Wei River valley. The Xianyang City Museum also displays a fine selection from the Yangjiawan tombs near the Changling. The Maoling Museum in Xingping County is known for unusual finds like those mentioned above; its best objects are split with the History Museum, Xi'an. The Tomb of Huo Qubing, which provides the setting for the Maoling displays, showcases the first large ensemble of stone sculpture associated with an imperial tomb complex and makes this a very rewarding visit.

SUGGESTED
READING

A good general source on tomb figurines is Virginia L. Bower, *From Court to Caravan: Tomb Sculpture from the Collection of Anthony M. Solomon* (2002); see also the catalogue *The Quest for Eternity* (1987) for objects from several Han imperial tombs. This author's essay in the latter, "The Qin and Han Imperial Tombs and the Development of Mortuary Architecture," pp. 16–37, was written before the Yangling discoveries. The annals of Jing Di (Emperor Ching) and Empress Wang are translated in Burton Watson, *Records of the Grand Historian* (1961), vol. 1, pp. 367–74 and 386–89.

Mount Xianggang: The King of Nan Yue 11

MUSEUM OF THE NAN YUE KING
GUANGZHOU, GUANGDONG
WESTERN HAN PERIOD, C. 122 BCE

Regional identity and local culture have long been part of the lives of people within China. The interacting cultures of the late Neolithic period (Ch. 3, Liangzhu) developed over time into the diverse Bronze Age states and cultures of the Eastern Zhou (Ch. 8, Jinan Cheng). Qin unification imposed administrative order on this diversity, and the two Han regimes that followed created mechanisms that promoted the economic, social, and cultural integration which created "imperial China." But throughout its long duration, the peoples of north and south continued to speak different tongues, rather misleadingly called dialects, and to enjoy life styles and customs that set them apart. They still do.

Thus it was a matter of considerable local pride in 1983 when archaeologists in Guangzhou (Canton) reported to the Cultural Relics Bureau in Beijing that they had identified a large, unmolested tomb of Han date in the very heart of their city. The extreme south, known as Lingnan (modern Guangdong and Guangxi, the drainage of the West River), has had a distinct identity from the late Neolithic and Bronze

Screen fitting

Age to the present. (Cantonese cooking remains one of the best known regional cuisines, after all.) The indigenous people, called Yue by northerners, were subjugated by a Qin army, and in 203 BCE their general, Zhao Tuo, claimed nominal independence. This kingdom, until it was conquered by a Han army in 111 BCE, enjoyed the benefits of a rich local economy, a prime location for trade with the southern ocean, and beneficial tribute relations with the Han imperial court in Chang'an. All of these cultural strands are represented by the unlooted tomb at Mount Xianggang.

Just south of the Guangzhou railroad station amid a bustling downtown district filled with high-rise hotels is a low ridge running east to west, the highest ground in the central city. Mount Xianggang ("elephant ridge") had been considerably shaved down by 1980 when a plan was announced to build four apartment blocks there. In June 1983, bulldozers were at work digging foundations when they ran into large blocks of stone, evidence of something man-made. Brought to the scene by a conscientious construction supervisor, archaeologists from the city and provincial museums probed the perimeter of these blocks and quickly identified a large tomb under them. They telegraphed Beijing for permission to start an excavation, and followed up with visits to the Institute of Archaeology, Beijing, which then became a partner in this work. In drafting their plan, they proposed to excavate the tomb chamber by chamber, working on the front areas first

Extravagant Burial

Section of tomb, Mount Xianggang

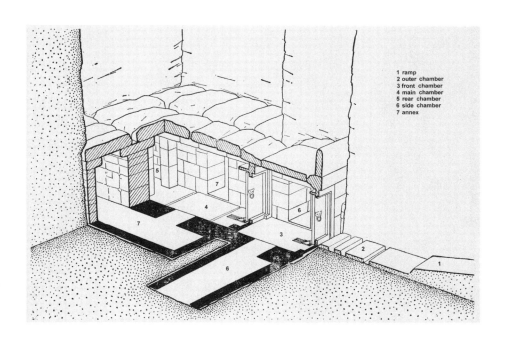

1 ramp
2 outer chamber
3 front chamber
4 main chamber
5 rear chamber
6 side chamber
7 annex

with a brief halt to review their results, and then embarking on the rear chambers, likely to be the richest. They also decided from the outset that the site was worthy of preservation as a museum. Hence their work was designed at every step to minimize damage to both structure and contents.

When excavation began in late August, a temporary shelter had been erected over the tomb, and separate teams were assigned to each chamber. About 17 m of earth had previously been taken off the ridge, so any evidence for a mound and shaft above was absent. The exposed chamber sat in soft bedrock, but had been constructed in ashlar masonry using harder red sandstone, imported from 20 km distant. Some 750 blocks of this stone, many quite large, were employed to build the walls and cap the chambers. Thus none of the spans were very great (most a bit more than 2 m); the largest capstone however weighed 2.6 tons. The tomb was not overly large, measuring only 11m along its north-south axis, and 12.5 m at its widest point. Some blocks had shifted, and a few had splintered and fallen in. The entrance ramp and passage were cleared rapidly, and the door to the front chamber was ajar enough to allow entry. But the doorway to the central coffin chamber was still shut, its panels locked in place from within. A lengthy series of meetings ensued among the excavation team and their leadership. How to open the chamber without damaging the doors or contents? After digging away the soft floor under the threshold, the excavators were able to crawl in for a reconnaissance. In the end, a skilled mason suggested simply digging under the pivot of one door panel to pull it out of position. The excavation concluded in early October, 1983. By 1988, a handsome site museum displaying the grave goods and protecting the stone chambers was opened to the public.

The hot, moist environment of Guangzhou took a heavy toll on the tomb contents. A wooden compartment in the entry passage, the many coffins, interior wooden door panels, and plank flooring had all decayed. Only traces of painting applied to the interior stone walls survived. Perishable objects like lacquer wares and textiles also disappeared.

A total of fifteen people were interred with the lord of this tomb, many in their own coffins: one in the outer passage; another in the wooden compartment outside the front doors; still another in the front chamber; one in the east front side room; seven in the west side chamber, and four consorts in the east side chamber. The lord of this tomb has been convincingly identified as the second king of Nan Yue, Zhao Mo, who died c. 122 BCE. The location of the Nan Yue royal tombs has been a mystery since the Han period, but only three of its five rulers are likely to have been buried in style. The tomb of the founder, Zhao Tuo, is still unknown; according to tradition, the third ruler's burial was looted.

The bronze and jade artifacts alone make this one of the richest finds in all Han archaeology, even now twenty years later. Like the Suizhou tomb of Marquis Yi (Ch. 7), the placement of grave goods was by function and type. The contents were a mixture of precious and high status objects, presumably possessions of the king, and local ceramics used specifically for burial offerings. The wooden compartment in the passage before the front doors held a large assortment of local hard pottery containing foodstuffs, as well as the bronze fittings for several umbrella-like canopies.

Within the first set of doors, the front chamber was occupied by a miniature chariot, but only its metal fittings remained. The east side room held chimes of bronze bells and musical stones, with many bronze vessels, considerable pottery, and fragments of lacquer. The opposite west side room was tightly packed with goods stacked in three layers on the floor. Many of these objects had been wrapped in silk now decayed. The mix included bronze food vessels and implements like ladles, braziers, and incense burners suggesting both distant and local sources. In addition, a variety of tools (both iron and bronze), weapons, and more chariot fittings were laid away, the latter in decayed lacquered hampers. This was also the source of more pottery, lacquer wares, glass paste objects, gold and silver, textiles, and ivory, although their preservation was generally poor.

The central chamber was given over to the two coffins and jade burial shroud of Zhao Mo, with ritual jades, especially disks, in abundance, weapons, and an elaborate screen for which the fittings survived. The highest concentration of jades worn as personal adornment were found here, as well as such unusual items as a covered silver dish of Persian origin. The four coffins in the east chamber are attributed to Zhao Mo's consorts; like him they were bedecked with pectorals of jade. The seven persons put to death in the west chamber, on the other hand, had no coffins, and only modest personal accessories. Finally, a large deposit of still more bronzes and some pottery nearly filled the rear chamber directly behind the coffins.

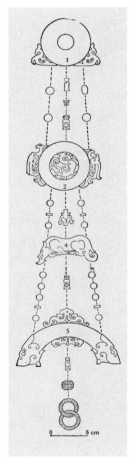

Jade pectoral

From a seal recovered in this tomb, we know that
Zhao Mo, the second king (*wang*) of Nan Yue, styled
himself the "Cultured Emperor" (Wen Di). From his
point of view, his burial on Mount Xianggang was an
imperial mausoleum, designed and furnished accord-
ingly. We as yet have no excavations of any Han
emperor's underground chambers, but more than
forty tombs of imperial princes have been opened.
The Han ritual treatises state explicitly that these
imperial siblings were interred with rites only a step
below those accorded the Son of Heaven. The treatises
detail features of their chambers, coffins, and shrouds,
many of which would have been prepared in imperial
workshops, such as the Artisan of the Eastern Garden.
Zhao Mo's tomb furnishings, while similar, surpass
those of most bona fide Han princes, but may still fall
short of the honors accorded an emperor.

The Western Han was an era of rich burials, and
several tomb plans were favored. Rock-cut tombs are
now documented at numerous locations: for example
in Hebei (the Han-era Zhongshan kingdom), in
Jiangsu (the Han-era Chu kingdom), and in Henan
(the Liang kingdom). Twin tombs near Mancheng,
Hebei are the best known, largely because when they
were opened in 1968 they yielded the first well-preserved examples of jade burial shrouds. (These have
since been displayed repeatedly in international exhibitions.) The tombs in Jiangsu and Henan are more
numerous, and follow more complex floor plans at
larger scale. Other Han imperial princes, however,
were buried in wooden chambers that required walls
of stacked, planed cypress timbers surrounding their

Han Princes

chamber and coffins. The best examples are near
Beijing (at Dabaotai, where there is a site museum, and
the newly reported Laoshan tomb in the Western
Hills) and at Changsha (see Ch. 12), where three
examples of this plan have been excavated. There are
also many examples of brick or brick and stone construction from several princely fiefs of the Eastern
Han period. At the time the Nan Yue tomb was
opened, less than half of these tombs had been
reported. Even today, and in spite of its relatively small
scale, the riches of Mount Xianggang surpass all other
Han burials.

The contents of this tomb also provide strong evidence for the material culture of the extreme south in
this period. The ceramics are characteristic local hard
pottery, well attested in Han cemeteries of lesser persons all over Guangzhou. Many of the bronzes, both
ritual types and practical ones, are well known
throughout the North, as are most of the weapons,
chariot fittings, and accessories such as mirrors. But
some metalwork is in the regional style associated
with Chu, while other objects would seem to be
southern castings, most notably the buckets with low
relief scenes of aboriginal people on their boats. Other
prestige goods, especially jade arcs and disks used for
pectorals, are common in the North, for example at
Mancheng and Xuzhou. Some examples here may
even pre-date Western Han. On the other hand, a jade
rhyton (drinking goblet) in the shape of a ram's head,
and a covered silver dish both seem to show Persian
traits (the latter matches other examples found in
Shandong). The likely vectors that sent such things to
the Nan Yue king and his tomb include the conquer-

Detail of boat scene

ing army of Zhao Tuo (perhaps with heirlooms), tribute received from Chang'an, trade and tribute from the coastal and southern ocean trade, and, of course, local workshops.

Since discovery of the royal tomb, archaeological investigations of Nan Yue have branched out to incorporate a garden in the royal palace, a boat construction site, and a major sluice.

Sima Qian wrote a brief history of "Southern Yue;" see Burton Watson, trans., *Records of the Grand Historian* (1961), vol. 2, pp. 239–50. Zhao Mo's burial suit and many jades are among the entries in Xiaoneng Yang, *The Golden Age of Chinese Archaeology* (1999).

SUGGESTED READING

12 Mawangdui: A Time Capsule from the Han

HUNAN MUSEUM
CHANGSHA, HUNAN
WESTERN HAN PERIOD, C. 186–168 BCE

While archaeologists generally must work with imperfect samples of compromised evidence, some discoveries stand at the opposite extreme. Burials, elaborate tombs in particular, are especially good ways to preserve the past, if they are not looted or damaged. And even though the material evidence from a tomb is admittedly a selective record of the past, favoring some things but excluding others, the amount of information to be gleaned from an intact, high status burial is impressive. Indeed, the effort that created the burial amounts to the creation of a time capsule. The Han tombs at Mawangdui fit this description.

The cultural relics system works well, but sometimes good fortune also plays a role in archaeological discovery. The double mound east of Changsha at Mawangdui was listed on the Hunan provincial historic register in 1956. Yet in 1971, without notifying the authorities, a hospital associated with the PLA began to dig away one slope with bulldozers. This continued until the day a worker's spade rammed into a wooden chamber and ignited a short-lived methane flame which erupted from the interior. Chastened, no doubt, by their experience, the PLA notified the

Hunan Museum. They fulfilled their duty by inspect-
ing the scene and beginning a salvage excavation, but
they failed to apply for permission from the National
Cultural Relics Bureau in Beijing. Only when word
leaked out that this tomb might hold a well-preserved
corpse did the required administrative machinery shift
into gear. The national bureau, under the watchful eyes

Excavation of tomb no. 3

of Premier Zhou Enlai and the Director of the
Academy of Sciences, Guo Moruo, then authorized
further work. They also supplied expertise from the
Institute of Archaeology, Beijing, still largely demobi-
lized in the later stages of the Cultural Revolution. The
excavation proceeded quickly, from January to late
April, 1972, with the participation of several dozen
units, government agencies including the local hospital,
construction bureau, even a middle school. A brief
report was published that year. The discoveries immediately became national and international sensations.

Marquis Dai

The mounds at Mawangdui took their name from a
prince of the tenth century (Ma Yin, hence "Prince
Ma's Mound"), although a local gazetteer claimed they
were tombs associated with two consorts of a Han
lord. In 1952, a team sent from the Institute of
Archaeology recognized that a low natural ridge had
been augmented by earthen mounds at two ends, and
were very likely late Zhou or Han tombs. After the
excavation of tomb no. 1 at the east end had begun, it
became apparent that its vertical shaft extended into
the original hillock to a depth of about 8 m. The
earthen mound built up later rose a further 8 m above
the ridge level. Four narrow terraces were cut into the
sloping sides of this shaft, giving mourners and work-
men a place to gather, and a sloping ramp was cut from
the north to bring down the coffin. The large shaft
(about 20 by 18 m at its top and 8 by 7 m at the base)
recalls the royal tombs of the Shang kings at Anyang
(Ch. 4), while the stepped terraces echo Chu practice
well known from Jingzhou (Ch. 8). Excavation of
tomb no. 1 led to discovery of two other burials, both
covered by the skirt of the mound over no. 1, and

hence earlier in date. To the west, centered under the second mound, tomb no. 2 was found at the base of a shallower shaft; it had been looted and was badly decayed. On the south slope of tomb no. 1, and at a similar depth, was tomb no. 3, with three steps at the top of its shaft and a ramp on the north. These tombs were excavated in 1973–74.

The chambers and coffins for these burials insured superior preservation. In each, the base of the shaft was covered with charcoal and sticky clay on which the runners and flooring of the chambers were laid. The chambers were assembled from large fir timbers, carefully cut and planed smooth. Seventy timbers created an outer chamber about 5 m by 3 m and 1.5 m in height in the case of tomb no. 1. (The largest timber at 4.8 m by 1.5 m weighed 1500 kg.) Harvesting this wood, preparing it, and then moving it into place suggest the level of expense and energy such tombs demanded. In plan, the chambers are subdivided by functions. The central area housed nested coffins,

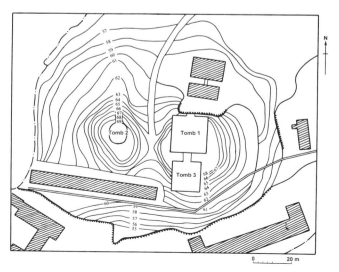

Plan of Mawangdui site

while the four side compartments held grave furnishings. All were covered with layers of ceiling planks. Additional sticky clay and charcoal then sealed the chambers. These compartments were almost airtight, with warm, moist atmospheres that permitted almost all their perishable contents to survive.

The coffins were rectangular boxes, deftly constructed using mortise and tenons, and then wrapped with silk bindings and sealed with lacquer. The middle two coffins of tomb no. 1 are also fine works of lacquer-painting, displaying panels filled with designs of apotropaic creatures of the underworld against a black ground or auspicious, numinous animals against a red ground, respectively. The inner coffin of tomb no. 1, on the other hand, was covered with silk. This inner coffin would have been carried from the family residence to the tomb site in the funeral procession by cart or chariot, pushed down the ramp, and finally lowered into the outer coffins already in the central compartment.

The corpse in tomb no. 1 was a woman of about 50 years of age, clothed in silk robes and slippers, and wrapped in twenty layers of shrouds (compare finds near Jinan Cheng; Ch. 8). Her hair piece was in place, and her tissues startlingly well preserved. The skin was pliant, joints flexible, and all viscera intact. An autopsy determined that her cadaver had, however, withered to a mere 34 kg, perhaps half her weight when alive, and found traces of a last meal, including melon seeds. The air-tight environment of the coffins and chambers seems to have been the main factor insuring her physical preservation. Bacteria, both aerobic and anaerobic, died early and decay was suspended. No efforts at mummification were detected. (The male corpse at the Jingzhou Museum is a parallel case.) Although tomb no. 3 was also intact, its corpse did not survive; only the skeletal remains of a 30 to 40 year-old male were recovered.

The lavish contents of the Mawangdui tombs are displayed in the Hunan Museum as brilliant examples of the material culture and artistic traditions of the south, specifically the state of Chu (see Ch. 8). Indeed lacquer wares, silk textiles and garments, wooden figurines, and texts written both on wooden or bamboo slips are relatively ubiquitous from late Zhou, Qin, and Western Han period tombs in Hubei and Hunan. Although these crafts flourished in other regions as well, today the best evidence for them is concentrated in this Middle Yangzi region at two major population centers (Jinan Cheng, Jingzhou, and Linxiang, ancient Changsha). Facilitating study of these objects are lengthy tomb inventories naming the investment of grave goods prepared for many tombs.

In addition to the lacquered coffins, two silk panels placed face down on the inner coffins in both tombs have gained wide attention. From their inventories, it would seem these were designated *fei yi* ("flying robes"). They were probably precursors of banners carried as part of the funeral procession (known from ritual texts as "name banners," *ming jing*) in later Han times. Both silk banners had darkened but were still intact. Each composition incorporates a depiction of the deceased in the stem surrounded by ascending dragons below a diagrammatic presentation of the heavens across the top. While various, sometimes contradictory readings of their subject matter have been offered, it is reasonably certain the banners in some way symbolize the cosmos and the fate of the soul

Wooden figurine, tomb no. 1

Fei yi *from tomb no. 1*

after death. The ascending dragons carry the deceased toward the gates of heaven, where a black sun–bird and toad in the moon occupy the far ends of each arm. Although a few other early banners exist, two late Zhou period examples from Changsha for example, none can match these two works of early painting in content or artistic quality.

The identity of the family buried at Mawangdui has been certain from the time tomb no. 1 was opened. Enough excavation had been done in Changsha to allow the archaeologists to date the tombs to the early Western Han period based on such features as the coffins, chambers, and burial goods generally.

Inscriptions on lacquer ware named a "Marquis of Dai" (Dai Hou), an aristocrat documented in the Han histories. The first Marquis, named Li Cang, was enfoeffed in 193 BCE, and was succeeded by a son, grandson, and great grandson. The latter two were not contenders for these tombs; the third marquis was buried near Han Chang'an, and the fourth, disgraced, lost his fief. The badly damaged tomb no. 2 was probably Li Cang himself (d. 186 BCE), since a seal bearing this legend was among its few, unlooted grave goods. The female buried in tomb no. 1 was most likely the wife of Li Cang, who died sometime later. The second male in tomb no. 3 was presumably a son of this couple who predeceased his mother. A slip from his tomb carried a date of 168 BCE. There is some dispute whether this could in fact be the second marquis, Li Xi, who died in 165 according to the Han histories. Thus, the Li family used the Mawangdui mounds from c. 186–168 BCE.

Changsha in the Han

The Mawangdui tombs are but three of an astonishing array of burials from the Western Han period excavated on both sides of modern Changsha. The Hunan Museum displays grave goods from tombs of higher ranking members of the Han aristocracy such as the tomb at Doubi Shan attributed to the consort of a Prince of Changsha, the tomb at Xiangbizui Shan attributed to Wu Zhu, another prince, and an even earlier consort's burial (lady Yuyang) at Wangchengpo. All three utilized a type of construction with hundreds of planed, fragrant cypress timbers on four sides of the chambers. (A similar tomb is on display at Dabaotai, Beijing.) As princes and their consorts, these nobles were two steps above the rank of Marquis Dai and family.

The finds at Mawangdui have been eclipsed in some respects by the sheer volume of excavations and a fairly steady accumulation of intact burials with well-preserved contents. But in one respect they remain unparalleled: the corpus of silk books, maps, and diagrams from tomb no. 3, the library of a son of Li Cang. The most famous of these texts are two versions of the *Laozi* (or *Dao de jing*), the classic of Taoism (Daoism). Among the other works are divination manuals such as the *Book of Changes* (*Yi jing*), a chronicle similar to the *Intrigues of the Warring States* (*Zhan guo ce*), two astronomical texts describing prognostication using clouds, stars, and comets, several medical treatises, an illustrated text showing breathing regimens, and maps, including both the region from Changsha to Canton and a military map. Tomb no. 3 held the largest selection of Han-era texts ever found in a single deposit. Like later documents from Dunhuang, Gansu, and Astana, Turpan, Mawangdui yielded an unprecedented treasure trove of primary sources.

SUGGESTED READING   Many of the myths that appear in the two funeral banners are translated and discussed in Anne Birrell, *Chinese Mythology* (1993). Three Mawangdui philosophical texts have been published: see Robert G. Henricks, *Lao Tzu: Te-Tao ching* (1989), Edward L. Shaughnessy, *I Ching: The Classic of Changes* (1996), and Robin D.S. Yates, *Five Lost Classics: Tao, Huang-Lao, and Yin-Yang in Han China* (1996).

Northern and Southern Dynasties

(220–588 CE)

The East Asian world changed in the third and fourth centuries CE. From the court-centered perspective of Chinese historians, the unity of the Han was lost as legitimate succession was contested, normative values suffered in the face of new religious and philosophical systems, and territories long considered the heartland were subjected to the rule of so-called barbarians. The varied names applied to the four centuries between the end of Han (220 CE) and reunification by the Sui (589) register these trends.

Over the long term there was a split in the control of Chinese territory between north and south. This fracturing leads to terms like "the period of division" and "Northern and Southern Dynasties." Ruling houses in the South claimed to be the orthodox successors to the Han, and made their capital safely across the Yangzi River at modern-day Nanjing (Ch. 14). The courts that controlled most of the south from the third century until 589 (Wu, Eastern Jin, Liu Song, Southern Qi, Liang, and Chen) also gain the sobriquet "Six Dynasties." On the other hand, the regimes that followed the collapse of Western Jin c. 316, dividing the map of North and Northwestern China, are the "Northern Dynasties," and were placed outside the line of legitimate succession by the Tang scholars who later compiled their histories. Since most of the Northern ruling families were of non-Han ethnicity, they have become known as "barbarian" regimes. In fact, most adopted many elements of Han culture, a trend labeled "sinification" by Chinese writers. (Cultural adaptation is actually a two-way street; back-and-forth exchange provides many of the fascinations and satisfactions of Chinese cultural history.) Whatever the hybrid culture of these Northern rulers, their descendants went on to reunify China Proper in the late sixth century.

In both North and South, Buddhism and a popular, religious Daoism became important cultural and social forces that affected the courts and their elites as well as a growing proportion of the common folk. The great monuments of the imperial capitals and extensive temple building transformed the material culture and archaeological legacy of this period. No account of Chinese archaeology can exclude the numerous finds of images (Ch. 15, Longxing Si) and relics (Ch. 19, Famen Si), as well as work at cave-chapels (Ch. 20, Mogao) in this period and the following Sui–Tang era.

Both barbarian customs and Buddhism, transplanted from India, highlight the manifold ways in which the great civilized centers of East Asia came into contact with cultures from Central and West Asia. The process had begun in the Han, but accelerated and deepened during this period. Non-Chinese objects (Sasanian silver, Roman glass), art motifs (the pearl roundel, lion, lotus), furnishings (the chair), dress and makeup, food (grapes) and music (the pipa), all came to the northern and southern courts. In subsequent centuries these things were regarded as integral parts of Chinese culture. China was created by Qin unification and Han consolidation. So too the culture of medieval times was the product of intense and complex interactions with a variety of neighboring peoples.

No volume covering this period has yet appeared in the *Cambridge History of China*. Aspects are introduced in two recent exhibition catalogues: Annette L. Juliano and Judith A. Lerner, eds., *Monks and Merchants: Silk Road Treasures from Northwest China, Gansu, and Ningxia Provinces, 4th-7th Centuries* (2001), and James C.Y. Watt, *China: Dawn of a Golden Age, 200–750 A.D.* (2004).

SUGGESTED READING

13 Luoyang: Nine Capitals

LUOYANG CITY MUSEUM AND
ROYAL ZHOU CHARIOT PITS
LUOYANG, HENAN

This guide features several of China's ancient capitals, and most of these cities flourished in more than one period. Luoyang exemplifies both characteristics: the metropolitan region was the location of five major sites that span the period from the early second millennium BCE through the end of the first millennium CE. Off and on for some three thousand years, the banks of the Luo River served as the capital of kings and emperors who ruled the central plains.

The two earliest major sites lie outside the present-day city to the east: Erlitou, in Yanshi county, a large site with a walled palace core that most Chinese scholars equate with the Xia (see pp. 9–12), occupies terrain on the south bank of the modern river, while the Shang wall at Yanshi (Yanshi Shang Cheng), west of the county seat, is considered an early Shang dynasty capital. Both of these locales are active today with important excavations. Even in the early Bronze Age the strategic importance and natural advantages of this region were recognized. Neither site was known to traditional scholars.

The three other major sites that occupied the Luoyang region are to the west, also on the flood plain

Mount Song Pagoda, Dengfeng

of the Luo River sheltered by the Mang Mountains across the north. The earliest was the initial occupation of an area known today as the "Han-Wei ancient city." Excavations of some of these walls revealed segments constructed in the Western Zhou period (c. 1050–771 BCE). Local scholars now claim this was the Western Zhou site called Cheng Zhou. A good deal further west, across the Chan River flowing from the north, is a second Zhou-period walled site known as the

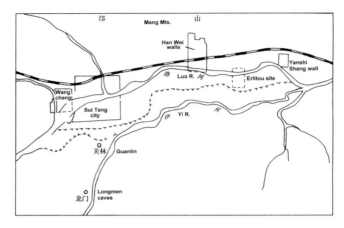

Map of sites near Luoyang

"Royal City" (Wang Cheng). It too was founded in the Western Zhou period, and became the seat of the Zhou kings after 771 BCE when they abandoned the Xi'an region (Ch. 6, Zhou Yuan). This city flourished during the Eastern Zhou period (770–256), but the fortunes of the Zhou were anything but robust. Regional lords assumed more and more power, and, while honoring the Zhou kings as "Sons of Heaven" in rhetoric, pursued their own aggrandizement in practice. The rise of the great states of Chu (Ch. 8, Jinan Cheng) and Qin (Ch. 9, Lishan) are notable examples.

After unification and the establishment of the Qin and Han capitals in the Wei River valley (Shaanxi), Luoyang again became the seat of a succession of dynasties ruling most of China Proper or its northern tier. The first imperial capital here was the Eastern Han (25–220 CE) city, the expanded "Han-Wei ancient city" built on Western Zhou foundations cited above, 15 km east of the modern city center. This same walled site then served the Wei state (220–265) of the third century, the Western Jin court (265–316), and, most notably, the Northern Wei (386–534). The latter unified the north in the early fifth century and relocated its capital to this region c. 493–95. Most of what survives on the ground at the "Han-Wei ancient city" dates from the ambitious rebuilding of the late fifth to early sixth centuries, when the Tuoba (Tabgatch) court adopted Chinese customs in matters of court ritual, dress, and even surnames, while also patronizing Buddhism on a lavish scale.

Luoyang was rebuilt once more in the early seventh century by the Sui (581–617), who made it their Eastern Capital, a status retained under the Tang (618–907). The Sui–Tang city was east of the modern city center, and straddled the Luo River, its overall plan indebted to Sui-Tang Chang'an (Ch. 17). Today a major expansion of the city is taking place here south of the river, atop the grid of the Tang Eastern Capital.

The North Bank of the Luo

The Luo River rises in Shaanxi and flows east and north 450 km across western Henan, merging with the Yi and eventually joining the Yellow River (Huang He) near Gongyi City. The five cities enumerated above arose in the northwest part of its basin, on the north, sunny bank of the river, and hence were named Luoyang. (The north bank of a river and south face of a mountain are both sunny, *yang*; the north slopes of a mountain and south bank of a river are both shady, *yin*.) The basin is sheltered by mountains on all sides, notably the Mangshan range on the north with elevations up to 400 m, Yique, site of the Longmen cave-chapels to the south, and Mount Song to the east, its main peak at 1440 m. The region has long been a crossroads.

In traditional history, the Duke of Zhou established two settlements in the Luoyang basin: Cheng Zhou (or Luo Yi), and Wang Cheng. Remnants of the vanquished Shang were also resettled here. The location of these two places is still debated: some scholars think the Royal City was within a larger Cheng Zhou, while others, especially Luoyang archaeologists, favor two locales as described above. Work along Zhongzhou Road in the 1950s revealed a large, square walled site near the Jian River, which was soon identified as the "Zhou Royal City." Some parts were protected within a park of the same name, and over the subsequent decades many discoveries of both the Western and Eastern Zhou periods have been reported across this part of the modern city, both inside and outside the ancient walls. The maximum area of this city during the Eastern Zhou period was 3.2 by 2.9 km, but only a few segments of its rammed-earth walls survive. Traces of palace foundations, granaries, workshops, kilns, and numerous burials have been cleared as modern Luoyang has grown, and new finds happen almost every year.

Eastern Zhou Royal Chariot Pits. Going east from the Jian River on Zhongzhou Road past Wangcheng Park and then the Luoyang City Museum, one comes to Wangcheng Square. This area, inside the east wall of the Eastern Zhou city, was redeveloped in 2002–3. The cultural relics work team located 397 tombs and 18 chariot and horse pits of the Eastern Zhou period during the initial phase of this project. One find attracted particular attention: pit no. 5, 42 m in length and 7 to 8 m wide, held seventy-six horses associated with twenty-seven chariots. The chariots were arrayed in two rows— one of twelve and one of fifteen—and their teams had two, four, or in one case six, horses. The horses had been put to death on the spot, and the archaeologists have carefully revealed their skeletons as well as the imprints of the wooden wheels, cabs, tongues, and yokes of the chariots. Since ritual texts claim a Zhou "Son of Heaven" (Tian Zi) drove a chariot with six horses, the authorities in Luoyang claim this could be a Zhou king's burial, although as yet no tomb has been cleared here (two large tombs with ramps nearby remain unexcavated as this is written). Since no Zhou royal tombs have ever been excavated at Luoyang, a discovery of this kind has considerable prestige.

Han-Wei-Jin Luoyang. The walls of the "Han-Wei Ancient City" encapsulate much of the urban history of this region. Starting from a rectangular walled area in early Western Zhou (perhaps Cheng Zhou?), this city was expanded first to the north in the Eastern Zhou period and again to the south during the Qin period. This new size and shape were inherited in turn by the Eastern Han (25–220) court, and served as its capital for almost two centuries. Although the south wall disappeared due to the northern shift of the Luo River, the other three city walls are intact, and many segments can be seen on the ground today. The walls enclose about 2.5 km east-west and about 3.5 km north-south. Two short-lived successor regimes reused the Han capital. In the first, the Cao Wei (220–265), a set of three fortified precincts was added at the city's northwest corner. In the second period, the Western Jin (265–316), the old Han palaces were rebuilt as a single walled area in the center of the city, the Luoyang Palace.

Little within these walls from the Han period has been excavated, but several suburban sites, now south of the river bed, produced important material. This area was dedicated to ritual precincts and altars of state, as well as the Imperial Academy. The Lingtai

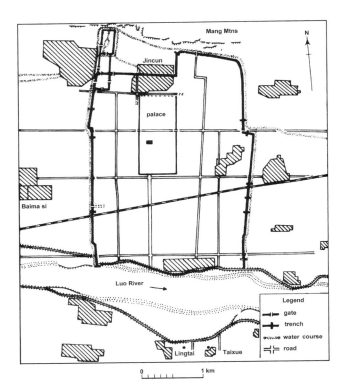

Plan of Han-Wei walls

(Numinous Terrace), an imperial observatory built in 56 CE, was among these structures, and its earthen core was cleared in the 1970s. The structure was built on a mound originally 50 m square and perhaps as much as 14 m tall. Traces of its lower two levels survived. A staff of forty court officials under the Grand Scribe observed the heavens and weather from this platform, informing the court of celestial portents as well as more mundane observations. The Taixue (Imperial Academy) was situated not far away, also now south of the river. Here the main finds have been broken fragments of the "Confucian Classics" inscribed on stone slabs in the Xiping era (c. 175 CE). These texts were written by Cai Yong, a leading scholar and calligrapher of his day, in clerical script. While the slabs were systematically destroyed at a later date, they have

been collected by antiquarian scholars since the Tang.
Work at the site in 1980 recovered more than 600
new fragments, most quite small.

Northern Wei Palace and Gates. The Northern Wei
court was ensconced in Datong, Shanxi, after its unification of the north in the early fifth century. The most
prominent physical remains here are the Yungang cave-
chapels, although in recent years several important
burials, including one imperial tomb, have been
reported. The Wei court sent officials to Nanjing to
study that city and its official architecture, so that when
it was decided to move to Luoyang, southern dynasty
architectural styles were adopted. Much of the plan of
the Eastern Han city was retained, but in the process of
rebuilding and refurbishing almost all the city was
reworked. The consolidated Luoyang Palace occupied
about one tenth of the walled area, measuring 1400 m

*Rubbing of Xiping era
classic (below left)*

*Yongning Si Pagoda
rendering by Yang
Hongxun (below)*

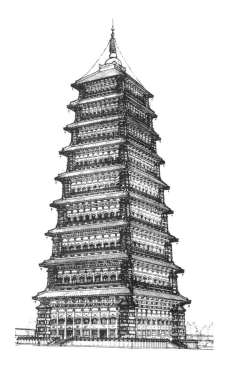

north–south by 660 m east–west. A major avenue running east–west crossed the palace, dividing it into two
zones: the south with major halls and the north for the
imperial harem and park. The much-damaged foundation of the main throne hall had a footprint 100 by 60
m. The city's principal thoroughfare, Tongtuo (Bronze
Camel) avenue, emanated from the palace south gate;
the major organs of state were laid out on its two sides.
That gate—the Changhe Men (Heavenly Gate)—has
been excavated. It was an impressive structure fronted
by two large towers that defined a square in front of the
main gate house, which in turn was set back from the
line of the palace wall. This is the plan of several later
gates, including the Wumen (Noon Gate) of the Ming
Forbidden City in Beijing.

Yongning Si. Among the few sites to survive above-
ground from the Northern Wei period is the ruined
great pagoda at Yongning Si. Constructed in 516 on
behalf of the emperor's mother, Grand Dowager
Empress Ling, this monument dominated the city
from its position southwest of the palace. Indeed, we
know that the imperial family took delight in ascending its heights to enjoy expansive views overlooking
the city and river. Today the ruins are near both the old
highway to Yanshi and the Long-Hai railroad, and can
be glimpsed from a nearby overpass. Plans are afoot to
open the site for display.

Surveys in 1963 first established the plan of this
temple, the grandest of its day in a realm with tens of
thousands of monks and nuns devoted to the dharma,
and 1300 temples in the capital itself. The plot is 300
m north–south by 212 m east–west; remnants of outer
walls, one corner tower, two gates, the pagoda, and
main Buddha hall have been plotted. Texts of the

period, such as *Record of the Buddhist Monasteries in Luoyang* by Yang Xuanzhi (Yang Hsuan-chih), give a detailed account of the temple and its architecture, which they compare to the imperial palace. These sources describe a nine-story, square wooden pagoda surmounted by a spire, but they differ on its height. The most ambitious estimate is 1000 Chinese feet (about 272 m), which seems highly unlikely. Chen Mingda, an architectural historian, suggests that if the height of each storey was twice the width of a bay, the pagoda would have risen to about 81 m with its spire, a more plausible but still impressive number. (The great Wooden Pagoda at Yingxian, Shanxi, dated 1056, is by comparison 67 m in height; see Ch. 21.)

The pagoda was supported by a huge subsurface foundation almost 2.5 m thick and nearly 100 m square. Centered on this terrace was the base of the tower, 38 m square faced with limestone slabs. Ramps on each side rose to this level, about 2 m above the ground. The structural heart of the building was four circuits of columns, three of them invested in solid unfired brick. This earthen and wooden spine may have risen as much as five or six levels. Niches set into walls between the columns of the fourth circuit housed a myriad clay images. About 1500 fragments were recovered in the 1979–81 excavations; many are on display at the City Museum. The fourth and fifth circuits of columns, spaced about 4 m apart, in turn delimited a gallery. A stairway rose here on the north to allow access to the upper stories. The ten columns of the outer, exterior circuit created a facade nine bays across, alternating three doors amid six windows. There also considerable evidence of a fire. Historical records report a conflagration caused by lightning in 534, from which the temple never recovered. Indeed, shortly thereafter, materials from the ruined pagoda were harvested for use in building the new Eastern Wei capital, Ye, in southern Hebei. It is unknown if the pagoda's relics remain.

The Luoyang region is well endowed with tombs of all periods, but especially the Eastern Zhou, two Han, Western Jin, and Northern Wei. The locations of the royal Zhou and imperial Han tombs, however, are fraught with uncertainties. The area of Jincun near the Han-Wei city walls is often suggested for the former, and the Mangshan range has a number of large mounds thought to date to Eastern Han. The Northern Wei emperors were buried on the highest ground north of the city and west of the Chan River. The Changling of Emperor Xiaowen (d. 499), who moved the capital from the north, and the Jingling of his successor, Emperor Xuanwu (d. 515), have been surveyed and the latter excavated. Several dozen tombs of all periods have been relocated to the Luoyang Ancient Tombs Museum, in proximity to the Jingling.

SUGGESTED
READING

For a general discussion of the capitals at Luoyang, see Fu Xinian, "The Three Kingdoms, Western and Eastern Jin, and Northern and Southern Dynasties," in *Chinese Architecture* (2002), pp. 61–89. Pre-Han sites are discussed by Li Xueqin in *Eastern Zhou and Qin Civilizations* (1985), pp. 16–36; the Han city is introduced by Wang Zhongshu in *Han Civilization* (1982), pp. 29–51. *The Record of the Buddhist Monasteries in Luoyang* (*Luoyang qielan ji*) by Yang Xuanzhi (Yang Hsuan-chih) has been translated into English twice; see Wang I-t'ung (1984) and W.J.F. Jenner (1983).

Nanjing: Imperial Tombs of the Southern Dynasties

NANJING, JIANGSU
SOUTHERN DYNASTIES, 4TH–6TH CENTURIES

The city now called Nanjing (Southern Capital) first gained the status of a national capital under Sun Quan, the founder of the Eastern Wu state, one of three successors after the Han disintegration c. 220 CE. Sun's occupation of his capital, called Jianye, was short-lived. By 280 a unified state named Jin (in retrospect, Western Jin) emerged with its capital once

Spirit path sculpture

again at Luoyang (Ch. 13). When, however, Jin itself
fell to internal revolt and external "barbarian" invasion
c. 316, the court took refuge in Sun's old capital,
renaming it Jiankang. Under this name the city served
as the imperial capital of ethnically-Han dynasties
until 589, a series known to historians as the Southern
Dynasties. In later times still other names were applied
to this city; it became Nanjing only when the third
Ming emperor moved his primary capital north to
Beijing c. 1421.

Traces of Jiankang

For centuries, scholars have gathered textual references
to Jianye and Jiankang, but physical traces of the capitals have been virtually non-existent. Various sources
suggest that the Southern court palaces and their walls
were between Zhongshan North Road and Taiping
Road, extending north to Beiji Ge. Only in 2001-
2003, however, did large-scale construction throughout the city coupled with targeted funding from the
cultural heritage authorities allow archaeologists to dig
to the earliest levels beneath downtown Nanjing. At
the site of the new Nanjing Library and at Xinpu New
Century Plaza, segments of roads, walls, foundations,
and wells were exposed, for the first time anchoring
the imperial sites of Jiankang in modern geography.
Among the finds was a north-south thoroughfare
divided into three lanes and paved with bricks dated
by their inscriptions to the 320s to 340s. This road and
another at right angles to it were 15 to 23 m wide,
flanked by drains. Piers for a wooden bridge were
uncovered outside an east-west wall parallel to the latter road. This wall varied in construction over time;
some segments were 12 to 13 m wide at the base and
faced with brick. Reinforced battlements were found

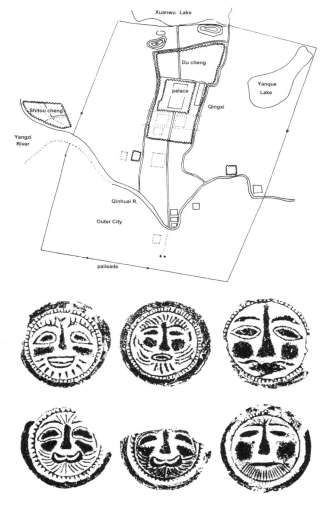

Plan of Jiankang in Southern Dynasties

Rubbings of tile ends

along one stretch, and a 10 m-wide moat lined with wooden stakes ran in parallel. In addition to such base-level traces of Jiankang, an abundance of tile ends and other building debris was collected. The capital (*du cheng*) in this era was a fortified palace (eventually with three sets of walls), encircled by rather less substantial earthen and wooden palisades connected to gates. In addition, fortified encampments flanked this palace-city on several sides. The most famous was Shitou

Cheng (Stone Wall) on the southwest, with command-
ing views from Qingliang Mountain down the Yangzi.

Outside the imperial capital were ritual precincts
required for a Son of Heaven. One of these was excavated in 1999 on the slopes of Zhongshan Mountain
due east of modern-day Nanjing. This mountain is
best known for the tomb of the first Ming emperor
(the Xiaoling of Zhu Yuanzhang, d. 1398; compare Ch.
24) and as the resting place for Sun Yatsen (d. 1923, the
Zhongshan Ling). Midway up the slope of the highest
peak (elevation 448 m), archaeologists found an
earthen platform lined with stones. This was an altar
complex established c. 459 by Emperor Xiaowu of the
Liu Song dynasty. The raised, level platform spreads
over an area of nearly 6000 sq m. The main section is
a terrace carrying four small altars, each about 20 m
square at the base and 1 to 2.5 m high.

Imperial Tombs

During the centuries of division more than seventy
emperors, their consorts, and princes were interred in
the outlying suburbs of Jiankang, in the modern districts of Nanjing, Jiangning, Gourong, and Danyang.
About thirty sites have been investigated; most are
assigned to rulers of the Eastern Jin, Song, Qi, Liang,
and Chen houses. While only eight tombs have actually been excavated, all of them have stone carvings on
the surface. These tombs share a common approach to
siting, plan, and construction that sets them apart from
contemporaries in the North at places like Luoyang.

The imperial tombs are located in the foothills of
the mountains that encircle Nanjing on several sides,
typically at elevations 70 to 100 m above sea level.
Based on the "frugal" approach of the Cao Wei
(220–265) and Western Jin (265–316), these are single-

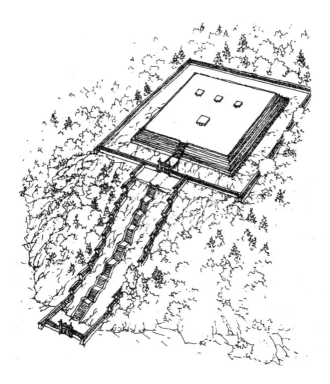

Rendering by Yang Hongxun of altar, Nanjing

chamber, vaulted brick tombs erected in large trenches dug from a slope. Trenches were as much as 20 to 40 m long, 8 to 10 m wide, and 5 to 15 m deep. A chamber, such as that at Huqiao, Danyang, may measure 15 m long by 6 m wide, with a height of 4.5 m. It consists of thousands of bricks carefully manufactured with impressed surface designs. These imperial tombs also have stone doorways featuring a semi-circular tympanum carved with a strut over the door. Covered drains collect and carry ground water away from the chambers; one extends 190 m down slope. Four of the excavated examples were given especially elaborate decor: bricks on facing walls that illustrate the "Seven Sages of the Bamboo Grove." These tombs seem to date on both sides of 500 CE, and represent a fascination with the ideals of reclusion and Neo-Daoism

*Rubbing of Wang Rong
of the "Seven Sages"*

exemplified by this cohort of eccentrics who lived
outside Luoyang before the loss of the North.
Unfortunately, the great majority of the imperial tombs
have been thoroughly pillaged, destruction that probably accompanied violent uprisings against the ruling
families. (The palaces of Jiankang met a similar harsh
fate when the Sui armies defeated the Chen in 589.)

The tomb locations described above were derived
from the Chinese practice of geomancy (*fengshui,
kanyu*), sometimes called the "science of siting." In the
belief that proper siting of a tomb (or house or city)
would have salubrious effects on the patrons and their
posterity, specialists were enlisted to locate environ-
ments with positive features: shelter on the north,
exposure to the sun on the south, good water drainage

and air circulation, and so on. These principles in fact embody sound environmental thinking; the advantages of drainage are obvious for a tomb site.

Southern Dynasties tomb chambers were approached by a long processional way, a "spirit path" that started on open, level terrain as much as 500 to 1000 m removed from the chamber. The approach was announced by a pair of gate towers flanking the path. A unique surviving example north of the city was excavated in 2000, although only its base was intact. In this case, the gate consisted of a pair of walls connected over the path. Like the high gate towers of a palace or city, this structure proclaimed the status of the site. The tombs also had timber-frame offering shrines for obsequies to the dead; like gates, none survive. What does remain at these thirty sites are large-scale stone carvings, the earliest examples (excepting a few Han pieces) of a major tradition of Chinese sculpture (Ch. 18, Qianling, and Ch. 24, Dingling). The earliest Nanjing imperial tombs of Eastern Jin (317–420) date seem not to have spirit path sculpture, and only one certain example of a Liu Song (420–79) tomb with stones is known. But for the Qi, Liang, and Chen rulers, ten sites offer evidence for this important mortuary tradition.

A spirit path is flanked by three types of stones: pillars, animals, and steles. Each type had roots in Han or earlier periods, but the Nanjing sites are the oldest concentrations of evidence for them. The pillars are monolithic columns with 24 or 28 fluted grooves installed in stone bases carved as curling animals. Some have stone caps with a crouching animal. Most pillars have small slabs of stone high up the shaft with short inscriptions that announce the identity of the deceased: "The spirit path of Taizu, Emperor Wen [of Liang]," for example. In some cases, the slab texts are written in both proper orientation (top to bottom, right to left) and as mirror-images, as if the deceased far behind could read from his vantage point (or as a contrast of *yin* and *yang*?) The best-preserved examples are at the tombs of Xiao Jing, the Liang Marquis of Wuping (d. 523) and Xiao Ji, the Liang Prince of Nankang (d. 527).

Spirit path animals have been given an assortment of names. Those at sub-imperial tombs are generally thick-bodied creatures with feline manes and lolling tongues. Those at imperial tombs, whatever their physique, have horns atop their heads and wings on their torsos. Single-horned creatures are usually called Bixie (literally "averter of evil"), while the double-horn species is known as Tianlu ("Heavenly benefit") or Qilin (misleadingly translated "unicorn"). Horned and winged creatures appear in various media in the late Zhou and Han periods, and Eastern Han and Jin tombs sometimes have small figurines of single-horned beasts that perhaps protected the tomb. Lions are not native to China Proper, but were widely used in Western Asia as royal symbols, for example flanking thrones, a role they fulfilled in Buddhist imagery and later Chinese imperial iconography as well. Thus there would seem to be a mix of native and foreign strands in this imperial funerary bestiary.

Steles are large flat slabs as much as 4 m tall mounted on a base carved as a tortoise, another example of foreign symbolism. (In ancient Indian cosmology, a great tortoise supports the world.) Slabs with funerary inscriptions are known from the Eastern Han period, although they have peaked tops. The curved tops of these steles are draped with intertwined dragons, their heads hanging down on each side. Their sides may also be decorated with a medley of fantastic auspicious and protective creatures. The stele texts serve as epitaphs that extol the pedigree and honors of the deceased. Their composition and writing were generally entrusted to court scholars known for their literary and calligraphic skills. Only a few examples remain *in situ:* for example, the tombs of Xiao Xiu (d. 519), Xiao Shen (d. 522), and Xiao Hong (d. 526), all Liang princes.

For an overview of the capitals and palaces of this era, as well as extant architecture, see Fu Xinian, "The Three Kingdoms, Western and Eastern Jin, and Northern and Southern Dynasties," in *Chinese Architecture* (2002), pp. 61–89. Objects from southern tombs are prominent in a recent exhibition: James C.Y. Watt, *China: Dawn of a Golden Age, 200–750 AD* (2004). Audrey Spiro, *Contemplating the Ancients: Aesthetic and Social Issues in Early Chinese Portraiture* (1990) is a stimulating discussion of the subject matter and broader contexts of the "Seven Sages" theme.

SUGGESTED READING

15 Longxing Si: Ritual Burial of Buddhist Sculpture

QINGZHOU MUSEUM
QINGZHOU, SHANDONG
N. WEI–N. QI, SIXTH CENTURY CE

In China, the archaeology of Buddhism encompasses several productive subfields. Relatively few ancient temples have been excavated, but some well-preserved sites actually allow well-considered reconstructions of lost structures (see the rebuilt hall at Qinglong Si, Xi'an, Ch. 17). More common have been excavations of pagoda foundations with their reliquary deposits rich in offerings (Ch. 19, Famen Si). Cave-chapels have also been systematically investigated by archaeologists, including structures in front of a cliff face (see Ch. 20). However, the most frequent Buddhist excavations have been caches of bronze or stone sculpture. These finds range from the occasional discovery by local farmers of a solitary image without context to deposits of hundreds of sculptures at abandoned temple sites. The richest of these finds in recent years was an extensive collection of stones recovered in 1996 at Qingzhou, Shandong.

These discoveries suggest that many unprovenanced Buddhist images now displayed in museums around the world emanated from similar finds made in the early twentieth century, when a demand for sculp-

ture first impacted the art market in China. Like ceramic tomb figurines, Buddhist sculpture was not highly prized by antiquarian scholars and collectors before their European and Japanese counterparts arrived on the scene. Given the frequency of such discoveries over recent decades, it is reasonable to assume that such finds, large and small, have been regular events. The dispersal of accidental finds unfortunately has continued in spite of legal prohibitions. Several museums in Taiwan and Japan have exhibited material that is believed to have issued from Shandong in recent years. This illicit traffic robs us of important data with which to assess and understand these finds. The Qingzhou discoveries illustrate the value of controlled excavation.

Buddha stele at Longxing Si Eastern Wei, h. 3.1 m

Images of the Buddha

In a mere week during October, 1996, the staff of the Qingzhou City Museum cleared a pit containing hundreds of fragmentary Buddhist images. The pit was first uncovered by construction equipment on a school athletic field next door to their institution. When the museum curators inspected the find, they reported a rectangular trench 8.7 m by 6.8 m with an opening 1.5 m below ground level. It had straight walls and square corners and reached a depth of 2 m. A narrow inclined ramp off center ran down from the mouth, and apparently had been in place when the trench was dug. The archaeologists speculate this was a convenience for moving heavy stones. The hundreds of stones were carefully arranged in east–west rows as three layers, most lying horizontal but some standing upright.

Detail of Buddha head

More complete images were clustered near the center; many disembodied heads were placed around the margins. A white Song porcelain jar was found amid the lowest layer of stones, and Song coins were also scattered about. Matting had been placed over the top.

The bulk (95 percent) of these fragmentary images was carved from local limestone. A few marble and granite examples were also found, the former perhaps imports from the Dingzhou region of Hebei province. A few iron, unbaked clay, fired ceramic, and wooden images were also noted, but most of them were in very poor condition. The preliminary census of the images arrived at the following counts: 153 Buddha heads, 51 bodhisattva heads, 36 torsos with heads, 200 headless torsos, as well as miscellaneous types. Since many heads cannot be matched to torsos, the actual minimum number of individual sculptures remains uncertain. One estimate suggests at least 320. All of these images were broken or damaged to some degree; some also showed traces of wear and repair. On the other hand, most do not bear common marks of iconoclastic destruction such as broken noses.

These stones range widely in date. Buddhist images may carry dedicatory inscriptions detailing the name of a donor, date, and circumstances. Here the earliest dated inscription is 529 (Northern Wei), the latest 1026 (Northern Song). The majority of the images can be dated by their style to the sixth century, in this region the Northern Wei, Eastern Wei, and Northern Qi dynasties; a modest number flesh out the following centuries. The Song porcelain placed at the bottom of the trench under the stones and the Song coins (the latest issued 1102–1107) suggest this deposit was installed after the beginning of the twelfth cen-

Standing Buddha
Northern Qi, h. 1.25 m

Standing Bodhisattva
Northern Qi, h. 1.36 m

tury, the late Northern Song period. Stratigraphy around the trench supports this estimate. Historical records of Qingzhou show that the location of the find was once a major Buddhist temple, Longxing Si, long defunct but a flourishing establishment during the Northern Dynasties and the Tang. Several other discoveries nearby have previously yielded similar sculptures.

How then does one explain this deposit? Archaeological context indicates a burial at the end of the Northern Song or somewhat later. At that time, the trench would have been within Longxing Temple, hence on sacred ground, several meters behind the temple's main hall. However, most of these broken stones date from the sixth century, some 500 years before their interment. The stones therefore lived aboveground for hundreds of years after their carving. Many retain gold paint and other pigments; some show differential wear to their surfaces; others have repairs attesting to care after damage. While periodic persecutions were a factor in the fortunes of Buddhism, it appears unlikely that persecution was the motivation for this burial. On the other hand, the care with which the stones were placed in the trench as well as the scattered coins and matting all suggest reverential disposal, presumably presided over by the monks of Longxing Temple. As Lukas Nickel has noted, the array of images is far too extensive and varied to represent icons from a single temple. He suggests that old images were gathered up from the wider area for disposal at the leading temple of the region. (This behavior would parallel the accumulation of worn-out Buddhist sutras and paintings placed in the "Sutra Cave" at Dunhuang, Ch. 20.) In fact, such activity is recorded in this area in this period.

Although many related finds have been made since the 1950s, only a few match the quantity and quality of the sculptures recovered at Qingzhou. In 1953–54, about 2200 stones, most fine-grained white Dingzhou marble, were unearthed at Xiude Temple in Quyang, Hebei. These small-scale images (most 30 to 50cm) spanned the Northern Wei through Tang periods, with a concentration in the Northern Qi (550–571) and Sui (581–617) periods. Some unfinished images and raw material suggest this may have been a regional production center. Many comparable images are in international museum collections; some likely came from this same source prior to its formal excavation. Also in the 1950s, another 200 images, most sandstone, were published from the Wanfo Temple site in Chengdu, Sichuan. They had been retrieved piecemeal since the nineteenth century, and were collected by archaeologists from the Sichuan Museum. These sculptures span the period from the Liu Song dynasty (420–479) through the Tang. The Wanfo Temple images have been especially valuable for understanding the development of Buddhist sculpture and iconography during the Southern Dynasties since Nanjing, the capital in this period (Ch. 14), has been bereft of similar finds. The Hebei and Sichuan caches thus allow scholars of Buddhism to track devotional trends in considerable detail. One can follow the rise of worship of Maitreya, the Buddha of the Future, and of Amitabha, the Buddha of the Western Pure Land in particular. In addition, each group supplies evidence for regional styles, and for interaction among regional centers. Both of these areas have produced still more recent finds; a small collection of fine sand-

Other Caches of Sculptures

stone carvings of the Southern Dynasties from Xi'an Road, Chengdu, was published recently.

In Shandong, the Qingzhou discoveries hardly stand alone. Several other locales not far from Qingzhou have reported multiple finds, now hundreds of images. At Boxing County to the northwest, the Longhua Temple has been the nexus for at least four major finds ranging from seventy images unearthed in 1976, to one hundred bronze sculptures found in an earthenware crock in 1983, to a variety of fragmentary stones. At Zhucheng County to the southeast, another ancient temple site produced 300 fragments interred in pits over an area of 80 by 100 m. Still more finds have been reported from Guangrao, Wudi, Gaoqing, Huimin, and Changyi. The circumstances attending these finds vary from seven or eight stones dug up by farmers to a cache of thirty-two images placed in the well of an abandoned temple. Some were neatly interred. Others show clear signs of iconoclasm.

Thus the Longxing Temple stones are but one example of a widespread phenomenon. Over time, local workshops must have produced stones and small bronzes in considerable quantities. These images were commissioned by patrons from many parts of society including officials and groups of laity. On occasion images were gathered up, perhaps for willful destruction, perhaps for reverent disposal. In Shandong the major persecution that would have damaged such images was c. 570 under the Northern Zhou, which extended its rule over what had been Northern Qi domains in that decade. The sites selected for burial were temple precincts, although today all traces of that edifice may be lost. Whichever set of circumstances led to burial, careful excavation of these deposits and study of the whole range of evidence gives modern scholars a glimpse into the sculptural workshops and devotional practices of medieval Buddhist communities.

The best overview of the Qingzhou finds is Lukas Nickel's catalogue, *Return of the Buddha: the Qingzhou Discoveries* (2002). Several images from Longxing Temple are discussed in Xiaoneng Yang, *The Golden Age of Chinese Archaeology* (1999). James C.Y. Watt, *China: Dawn of a Golden Age, 200–750 A.D.* (2004) features Buddhist stones from Sichuan. For a wide-ranging discussion of the role of Buddhism in Chinese history, see Jacques Gernet, *Buddhism in Chinese Society: An Economic and Social History from the Fifth to the Tenth Centuries* (1995).

SUGGESTED READING

16 Jiaohe: Ghost City

TURPAN, XINJIANG
LATE BRONZE AGE THROUGH TANG
3RD C. BCE–10TH C. CE

The Turpan Basin, with terrain at 150 m below sea level, is the second lowest region on earth after the Dead Sea. Bordered by the Flaming Mountains across the north, it is a land of fertile oases watered by underground channels (*karez*) that crisscross the desert. From the Chinese perspective, Turpan first appears in history during the Western Han period, with conflict between the new imperial state and the Xiongnu

Stupa in Great Temple

steppe confederation usually equated with the Huns.
A kingdom called Jushi occupied the Turpan Basin at
this time. For much of the next two centuries the
rulers of Jushi surrendered alternately to Han and
Xiongnu armies that arrived at their doorstep as they
contested control over the thirty-six states of the
"western regions," the Han term for the greater Tarim
Basin. The *Han History* of Ban Gu (c. 120 CE) reports
that: "The seat of the king's government is at the town
of Jiaohe. The river divides and flows around the walls,
and the town is therefore named 'connected rivers.' "

At the end of the nineteenth century, Jiaohe (or
Yarkhoto in Uighur) first appears in world archaeology with investigations by European and Japanese
explorers. They found a true ghost city 10 km west of
the city of Turpan, an abandoned site of ruined
earthen architecture atop a terrace still defined by the
"connected rivers" that inspired its name. Today, Jiaohe
is the focus of extensive efforts by the Chinese and
Japanese governments and UNESCO to preserve and
excavate its heritage. Their project has made Jiaohe
one of the most powerful experiences of the past
available to the traveler in China today.

The City

Jiaohe occupies an earthen terrace in the shape of a
willow leaf about 30 m above the split channels of the
Yarghul River, oriented northwest-southeast. At its
widest this table land is about 300 m across, and the
built-up portions of the site occupy about 1000 m of
the total length of 1700 m. The city's elevated position
created natural defenses, although a section of wall was
built along part of the west edge. Three gates—south,
east, and west—controlled access. Both the south and
east gates were steep climbs difficult for animals and

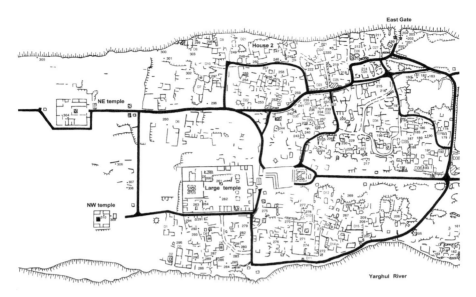

Plan of Jiaohe

carts to ascend, while the west gate was probably restricted to foot traffic. Visitors today climb a gentle ramp next to the proper south gate. The city's main north-south artery runs from this point to the largest surviving Buddhist temple. On both sides of the road extensive areas were once developed but subsequently leveled, leaving few early structures. An administrative complex excavated recently on the east side was a large, self-contained courtyard that quartered the Tang garrison in the seventh century. Moving north, also on the east side, are residential zones, with courtyard dwellings that open onto lanes perpendicular to the main road. The most important of the fifty Buddhist sites are arrayed across the north, including a large monastery with stupa, two smaller temples (designated northeast and northwest, respectively), and the remarkable "forest of stupas" (*ta lin*) still further north. A cemetery fills the north end of the terrace.

All the ruins seen today in a walking tour are earthen. Their construction falls into several main types, with variations. Many of the earliest and largest structures including the high walls that line major roads and lanes were carved from the original surface of the table land. Excavating the earth left large channels below ground level that became a road bed or the yard of a large building. This technique was labor intensive and made further alterations difficult. In recent centuries many of the early structures created in this way were damaged by local farmers who hauled away the soil as fertilizer for their fields. Another important construction method was rammed earth whereby loose soil was compacted to build up walls. This technique could supplement the first method to fill in the smaller features of a building. (This same technique created most city walls, foundations, and burial mounds in China Proper; p. 94.) Also widespread was a process in which mud was piled up in layers and then trimmed to shape. Finally, some sun–dried brick was also employed, although this may only have

Forest of Stupas

started late in the history of the city. Huihu (Turks) masons certainly employed it for vaulting in the ninth century. Today, such brick is also used in restoration. In a very real sense, therefore, the Jiaohe ruins are a great dilapidated work of earthen sculpture, both remarkably durable in the aggregate and fragile in the case of individual structures. Do not climb on these ruins!

The Buddhist monuments of Jiaohe are its most impressive features. Monasteries, like the "northwest temple," were built as walled, square or rectangular structures facing south. Cells within the walls on both sides typically flank a central yard. Several of these temple blocks are fronted by paired stupas, either outside their main gate or inside their yard. At the rear and on axis is usually a large hall or a stupa, or both, with a terrace, the latter square in plan with a passage for circumambulation around the base. None of these buildings truly survives intact; their structures are generally devoid of whatever skin they once had. A few temples have niches on the sides of a stupa showing traces of wall painting or sculpture. (A replica of the "small northwest temple" giving a sense of its original appearance has been constructed near the visitor's parking lot.) The 101 stupas of the Forest of Stupas still impress a visitor and are well worth the extra hike. The main stupa here was built on a square base with a large central tower and four smaller towers disposed at the corners. Surrounding it are four plots, each with twenty-five small square stupas in five rows of five. Early records indicate these were two-story towers like the five spires of the center. All of these stupas must have been faced with clay architectural moldings and figural reliefs in the manner of the better known Gandharan sites of Pakistan and Afghanistan.

The Xinjiang Uighur Autonomous Region is now considered an inseparable part of the People's Republic, but it was not always so firmly within the orbit of China. Xinjiang only came into existence when the Manchu Qing government annexed the region; it was first designated as a province in the late 19th century. As an autonomous region since the 1950s, the Beijing government has formally recognized its once predominant, non-Han population (the Uighur Turks; in Chinese Wei-wu-er) as deserving preferential treatment in matters of language, religion, and population policy. Over the long span of Chinese imperial history, however, the interaction between Chinese regimes and the populations of the area now called Xinjiang waxed and waned. Moreover, those populations have themselves changed over time, as several great world civilizations (India, Persia, the Turks, and Mongols) spread across Central Eurasia. The Turpan Basin in general and Jiaohe in particular are a microcosm of these complex, intertwined cultural relations.

Before the arrival of Han cavalry, the basin was home to an Iron Age population, some "Europoid" in physical features, others akin to the indigenous peoples of North China. The *Han History* says little of the culture of the Jushi kingdom with its seat at Jiaohe beyond enumerating the numbers of households and men at arms, and the titles of its officials. Cemeteries excavated in recent years on a terrace north of the city represent the Iron Age residents of Jiaohe, and perhaps were the Indo-European (Tocharian) speakers many scholars believe lived here. The Han exercised intermittent control over Jushi, and posted military forces in the area to keep the northern route around the

The Western Regions

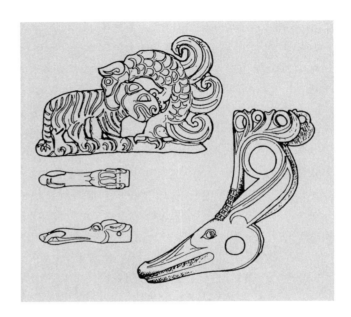

*Grave objects at Jushi
Cemetery*

Tarim Basin open. The great army that assaulted
Ferghana (Dayuan) passed through Jiaohe. As Han
power declined in the third century CE, many ethnically Han people from the northwest Gansu corridor
migrated to the Turpan Basin, which was under the
control of several Northern Dynasties. The city supported an extensive cemetery with their remains on a
terrace to the west. Under the rule of the Qu family,
an independent Gaochang state controlled the basin
between c. 498 and 640, and the region sustained a
flourishing Buddhist culture. Tang armies occupied
the area in the latter year, and for a decade and more
the Turpan area, specifically the Gaochang site to the
east, was the seat of the Anxi Protectorate, the military
command that controlled the whole of the Tarim
Basin. Jiaohe was reduced to a county seat of the
"Western Prefecture" during this time, and soon
hosted its military headquarters. Later in Tang, central
control wilted, and eventually (c. 866) the Huihu

Turks gained control of Gaochang and with it Jiaohe. They held on to this region until the Mongol armies of Genghiz Khan arrived in the thirteenth century. Jiaohe bears scars from this episode as well, specifically a cemetery of children put to death by the Mongol army.

Turpan is home to two ruined city sites. The second, Gaochang (in Uighur, Qocho), is 50 km east of the modern city. In general preservation here is less impressive than at Jiaohe. If the latter now is mostly Tang-era ruins, the Gaochang site is what remains after the devastation of the Huihu city wreaked by the Mongols. However, Gaochang is larger, 5 km on a side, and some of its monuments, like the so-called khan's fort and several temples, are rewarding. The Astana cemetery outside the city on the north has hundreds of graves, many from the period of the Tang Western Prefecture. As true elsewhere in Xinjiang, the extreme aridity of the climate has preserved perishable objects as well as human corpses. Extensive paper documents, many textiles and articles of clothing, even dried pastries, have been recovered from these tombs; several are open.

The Turpan Regional Museum provides a thorough picture of local history in displays drawn from both city sites. Many Turpan artifacts have also been sent to the Xinjiang Museum in Urumqi. The Jiaohe site museum at the south gate displays an informative model of the city. The Bezeklik cave-chapels are situated in a spectacular gorge north of Gaochang and Astana, and should not be missed.

Little in English describes Jiaohe. The *Han History* account of Jushi is translated by A.F.P. Hulsewé in *China in Central Asia: the Early Stage: 125 B.C.–23 A.D.*

SUGGESTED
READING

(1979). The dessicated corpses of Turpan are treated in two readable accounts: Elizabeth Wayland Barber, *The Mummies of Urumchi* (1999), and J.P. Mallory and Victor H. Mair, *The Tarim Mummies: Ancient China and the Mystery of the Earliest Peoples from the West* (2000).

Bezeklik cave-chapels

Sui and Tang

(581–906)

The medieval empires—Sui and Tang—are often compared to their predecessors, Qin and Han. Like the Qin, Sui (581–617) was a short-lived dynasty that achieved unification after a period of division. Like Han, the Tang (618–907) inherited most of what its predecessor, Sui, had accomplished, and then went on to consolidate and strengthen that imperial order for the long term. Apt as these points of comparison may be, the parallels disappear when considered further. The Sui and Tang royal houses were linked intimately; both were founded by generals from elite northwestern families, and belonged to a common peer group with ancestors who were "non-Han." By contrast, the upstart commoner Liu Bang who became the founder of the Han had nothing in common socially with the Dukes of Qin, although both dynasties are considered to be (ethnically) "Han." Similarly, the world of Sui and Tang had changed markedly from the world of the first centuries CE. New states and regional powers had arisen on the frontiers: Turks across the north, Tibetans to the west, and a powerful Korean kingdom to the northeast. With the exception of the Xiongnu, no great powers confronted Qin and Han on their periphery.

By lumping Sui and Tang together, and by setting aside the vicissitudes of dealing with their powerful neighbors, we project an aura of might, cosmopolitanism, and high cultural achievement onto this period of more than three centuries. Tang is almost always characterized as a great or golden age, largely because of the high repute of some of its rulers, like Taizong (r. 626–49) and his minister Wei Zheng, and the cultural glories of the age: the great capital, Chang'an (Ch. 17), architecture, poetry, calligraphy, and splendid painting and sculpture. The cultural high points were real, and some survive for our inspection. But the historical circumstances that produced these assets were more complex. The great capital and many other monuments were constructed during an initial creative phase of building, from the Sui through the late seventh century. Court politics turned deadly and desperate under the notorious Empress Wu, who declared herself an emperor and changed the name of the dynasty for a time. Revival of the Tang house was short-lived, culminating in a disaster of great magnitude, the rebellion of An Lushan and Shi Siming which sent the emperor fleeing to Sichuan in the mid-eighth century. The power of the Turks, especially the Uighurs, cost Tang dearly, leading to widespread devastation in the two capitals. The persecution of Buddhism in the mid-ninth century also took its toll. By the late Tang period, regional military commanders ruled most of China Proper and the court was weak. Viewed as a whole, more than half of this supposed golden age was an era of misery for many of its people. Still, some of the best poetry emerged amid such duress.

In recent times, the Tang has also been celebrated as the age when the "Silk Road" flourished. Its cosmopolitan capital was at the receiving end of foreign cultures, their music, art, cuisine, and costume. Archaeology has been especially successful at exemplifying what is known from textual sources with material evidence, from silks at Turpan to silver vessels in Xi'an. But East Asia and China had always been tied to the cultures of the west, and after the advent of Buddhism in the period of division, had maintained steady links with South Asia as well. A cosmopolitan society and culture were already in place during the Northern Dynasties. What distinguishes Tang is the prominence of foreign things in elite, capital society, and their representation in Tang sources, including archaeology.

SUGGESTED READING

For all things Tang, the source of choice is Denis Twitchett, ed. *The Cambridge History of China, vol. 3, Sui-T'ang China, 589-906* (1979). For a wide-ranging discussion of the role of Buddhism, see Jacques Gernet, *Buddhism in Chinese Society: An Economic and Social History from the Fifth to the Tenth Centuries* (1995). Edward Schafer's *The Golden Peaches of Samarkand: A Study of T'ang Exotics* (1963) offers short essays on the cosmopolitan Tang world.

17 Chang'an: A Chess Board Grid

XI'AN, SHAANXI
SUI AND TANG PERIODS, C. 581–906

Walking the busy streets of modern Xi'an, passing KFC and McDonalds, there are nonetheless many signs of the city's past. The modern road grid of Xi'an still retains the imprint of the avenues and wards that comprised the Tang capital. The massive gray-brick Ming walls (14th–15th centuries) that surround the old city center trace the path of the Tang Imperial City walls and even embrace their original earthen cores and gates. Two authentic monuments from the Tang— the Great Goose and Little Goose pagodas—mark the skyline. Ersatz Tang sites are also in fashion, from the credible reconstruction of the halls at Qinglong Si in the southeast to looser evocations in contemporary buildings including the Shaanxi History Museum. And of course there is a steady diet of advertising signage with evocative images of graceful Tang dancers twirling their long sleeves.

Tang Chang'an, which by no accident shares its name with the Western Han capital, most probably was the greatest city of its day, the seventh and eighth centuries, in both area and population. It was surely the most ambitiously planned city of pre-modern times.

Great Goose Pagoda

While other early capital sites are featured in this guide, none of them offers the breadth and depth of sites and resources for understanding a great cultural moment that Chang'an (Xi'an) does. Luoyang (Ch. 13) and Nanjing (Ch. 14) come closest, and for similar reasons. Like Xi'an, they have seen much modern growth and hence salvage archaeology that has uncovered their past. And they were studied by antiquarian scholars in pre-modern times; thus some of their sites and monuments were set aside for veneration long

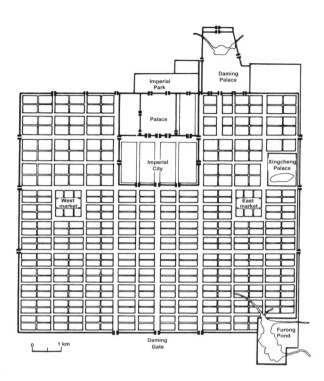

Plan of Tang Chang'an

ago. And, like Chang'an, they are depicted in traditional history, literature, and art. Chang'an nonetheless exceeds all other early capitals for the number of windows that open onto its past.

"Eternal Peace"

Studying the layout of Chang'an leaves no doubt it was a rigorously planned city, embodying both the ideology and practical agendas of its imperial patrons. We have the name of its principal designer, Yuwen Kai, and the date construction commenced (from the sixth lunar month of 582, the second year of the Sui). Named initially Daxing Cheng (Great Renewal City) after the fief of the Sui founder, the city retained its status under the Tang, but was renamed Chang'an (Eternal Peace) in 652 to evoke the glories of Han. The city was first and foremost the seat of the Son of Heaven, the ruler of the world and a social class of one. (Although in early Tang, aristocratic families of the northwest still saw themselves as peers of the imperial clan.) The emperor's palace determined the central axis of the city, its south gate opening to an avenue that continued for over 5 km to the outer wall's central portal, the Mingde Gate. The palace was placed against the city's north outer wall, and connected by gates to an imperial park beyond. The ruling sovereign was to occupy its central precinct, while the heir was to inhabit the much smaller eastern area and palace ladies were ensconced in a more commodious western section. Fronting the Palace astride the axis was the Imperial City, a little larger, home to the ministries of state, the imperial ancestral temple, the imperial guards, and other agencies of court business and ceremony. A great east–west avenue between the Imperial and Palace cities served as an approximation of a public square, with a width of 220 m. Today the Shaanxi provincial government center stands near this site.

Mingde Gate rendering by Fu Xinian

Over time, however, the locus of imperial activity shifted, first by the late seventh century to higher ground outside the north wall to a vast palace called the Daming Gong, and then, in the eighth century to the city's east side, the Xingcheng Gong. Both of these palace complexes incorporated extensive garden- or park-like settings, with formal ensembles of buildings as well as informal halls. Thus the emperors could both preside at court and relax without leaving their palaces. Movement between these locales was facilitated by a wall built parallel to the city's proper eastern wall. Imperial parties could pass unobstructed and unobserved between the two; this wall was later extended further south to Furong Pond at the city's southeast corner. It became a virtual recreation center in the last days of the capital. Tang poets describe its attractions and elegant denizens.

Most of the area within the city walls—9.7 km east-west by 8.6 km north-south—was subdivided into over one hundred wards. Eleven avenues running north-south sliced the city into ten vertical columns, while fourteen cross streets defined thirteen rows of horizontal blocks. To paraphrase a Tang poem, this is a city laid out "like a chess board," its wards "like neat garden plots." The widest avenues connected opposite gates, three each on east, south, and west; they ranged in width from 40 to 100 m. The broadest avenue at 155 m linked the Mingde Gate on the south to the Red Bird Gate of the Imperial City. Lined by water ditches and shade trees, the center of this thoroughfare was a lane reserved for imperial traffic. The wards were themselves walled and gated, usually with a grid creating four blocks and openings on each cardinal direction. The largest wards flanked the Palace and Imperial

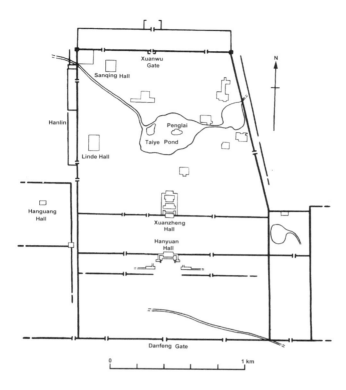

Plan of Daming Palace

cities in the north; the smallest were four columns south of the latter, with only east and west gates. Wards were usually subdivided into sixteen blocks; some temples or mansions of the elite might occupy several. We know the addresses of many famous figures of the Tang, at least down to their ward and block. The higher ground of the eastern half of the city was preferred by the well-to-do. Some of the southern wards were considered country retreats because the area remained undeveloped.

Two great markets took over double wards on the city's east and west sides, south of the Imperial City and convenient to the central gates on both sides. Hundreds of merchants had shops and workshops lining the lanes of these markets, which were supervised

closely by the imperial authorities. At the center of the
nine blocks inside each market were the offices of the
price administration. We have fairly detailed information about the merchants, their products and prices
thanks both to government records and the jottings of
Tang writers. The western market was especially noted
for its cosmopolitan population and many resident foreign merchants. When Tang artists wished to depict
visitors from abroad—Persians, Sogdians, Tibetans,
Turks—they had only to take up a seat in a wine shop
in the market and watch the crowds surge by.

The plan of Tang Chang'an was devised from
study of earlier capitals, but also rationalized by invok-
ing symbolic and ideological principles. The designers
studied Luoyang of the Northern Wei (Ch. 13) and Ye
from the Northern Qi period. They found precedents
for residential wards in both and for a north-central
palace of the Son of Heaven in the latter. They also
took advantage of six natural ridges running north-
east-southwest across the city, equating them with the
six lines of the hexagram *qian* in the *Book of Changes*
(*Yi Jing*) Thus certain ridges (lines) were deemed
appropriate for certain functions, as explicated in
scholarly commentaries to the *Changes*. They also
knew that the canonical "royal city" plan prescribed a
square city oriented to the four cardinal directions,
with three gates per side. On a more practical level, the
city's designers utilized a module of 2800 by 3300 m
derived from the Palace and the Imperial City as their
unit for laying out the site. With this unit, the city took
its overall shape from a five by three grid. The
Daxing/Chang'an plan that emerged was widely
influential, first in Tang (for the Eastern Capital,
Luoyang) and also in other parts of East Asia, includ-

ing modern-day Korea and Japan. Later Chinese capitals reacted to the precedent of Chang'an, for example Northern Song Kaifeng and Yuan Beijing (Ch. 23).

None of the major palatial and temple structures of Tang Chang'an survive today. The city was burned and depopulated in the early tenth century, and building materials—wooden columns and beams, paving and roof tiles—were harvested and transported east to Luoyang, then being rebuilt as the capital of a short-lived regime. A much smaller city occupied the site in later centuries. The Yuan city was more or less the area of the Tang Imperial City; while Ming Xi'an was an expanded version of the same, its walls pushed further north and east. As a result, most of the Tang sites excavated in recent years have been outside the city center as delimited by the Ming walls for a thousand years, and thereby survived to the twentieth century (where they have faced a serious threat from the rapid growth of the modern city). The two great palace complexes (Daming and Xingqing) have been protected since the 1950s; the latter is a pleasant city park, the former a major focus of archaeological investigation. Recent campaigns at Daming Gong have unearthed the great man-made lake that was the focus of its rear park-like precincts. One of the most important Tang ritual sites, the Altar of Heaven, has also miraculously been protected on the grounds of Shaanxi Normal University. Several city and palace gates have been cleared, as have portions of several wards and the two markets. The most ambitious effort to rebuild on a Tang site is the Qinglong Si, where a main hall has been reconstructed through the efforts of Chinese and Japanese Buddhists. The temple is revered as the place where

Tang Monuments

the Japanese patriarch and culture hero Kukai studied esoteric teachings. Outside the city, several other palaces have been excavated, notably the Huaqing Chi, a hot springs retreat favored by Emperor Minghuang and his notorious consort, the Lady Yang Guifei, in Lintong, near the Lishan necropolis (Ch. 9).

More direct experience of the Tang city comes from visiting the two surviving brick pagodas. The larger, known as the Great Goose Pagoda (Dayan Ta, but formally the Ci'en Si Pagoda), was built by Emperor Gaozong in 652 as a five-story wooden structure on behalf of the intrepid Xuanzang, recently returned from India. It was rebuilt by the Empress Wu in 701–704, and remodeled since, assuming its seven-story brick form. The Little Goose Pagoda (Xiaoyan Ta) is within the grounds of the Jianfu Si, and dates to 707–709. Its narrow-set eaves and curved profile contrast with the ponderous Great Goose. Both pagodas are now part of large temples where all else is of much later date and appearance. The Great Goose rises near a new public square and commercial district, much of it built to evoke a Tang ambience.

Another way to experience Tang Chang'an is through objects recovered from sites around the city. The most famous cache of Tang gold and silver before the Famen Si finds (Ch. 19) was dug up at Hejia Village, a residential area of Xi'an once within the Tang walls. A selection from the contents of two large crocks found by accident in 1970 is generally on display at the Shaanxi History Museum. Likewise, a deposit of elegantly carved white marble Buddhist sculpture from the Anguo Si, retrieved in the 1950s on that site, are usually displayed in the sculpture galleries of the Beilin, the "Forest of Steles" that occupies the

old Confucian Temple. The Sui-period sarcophagus of the nine-year-old Li Jingxun whose tomb was opened in the 1950s on the city's west side is also featured here. The Beilin is renowned for its calligraphic monuments. Among its Tang examples are the 114 stone slabs used for the Kaicheng Classics (837), the Confucian curriculum totaling an estimated 555,000 characters, the *Classic of Filial Piety* (*Xiao Jing*) written out with his own commentary by Emperor Xuanzong (745), and the so-called Nestorian Stele (781), which records the Tang court's recognition of this heretical Christian sect.

Ritual hall at Qinglong Si

Victor C. Xiong, *Sui-Tang Chang'an: A Study in the Urban History of Medieval China* (2000) offers a thorough introduction to the city and all of its parts. Edward Schafer's *The Golden Peaches of Samarkand: A Study of T'ang Exotics* (1963) makes frequent references to the life of the capital.

SUGGESTED READING

18 Zhaoling and Qianling: The Tang Imperial Tombs

LIQUAN AND QIAN COUNTIES, SHAANXI
TANG PERIOD, 7TH CENTURY

The largest and most imposing imperial burials ever constructed commemorate the rulers of the Tang dynasty. In sheer scale, the two largest Tang imperial necropolises dwarf anything before or after. The Zhaoling, the tomb precinct of Li Shimin (Taizong, d. 649) is 60 km in circumference. Within lie 200 satellite burials of imperial family members, notable officials, and generals. The Qianling, the joint burial of Li Zhi (Gaozong, d. 683) and Empress Wu (d. 706), is 40 km around, although by comparison it has fewer satellite tombs. Thus both are larger in the area they enclose than the Tang capital Chang'an (at 36 km around the outer walls). By contrast, the walls of the Lishan necropolis are 6.2 km in circumference; the Ming valley has a perimeter of 20 km.

The Tang court instituted strict sumptuary regulations governing every aspect of an official's or a commoner's life. Thus dress, chariots, houses, and tombs with their furnishings were all graded by the social rank of the individual. These stipulations enforced social distinctions and dictated economic activity. Epitaphs in Tang tombs generally record the official titles of the

deceased, and in practice the size and furnishings of these burials usually correlate well with prescriptions laid out in Tang treatises on such matters. The imperial family, however, as a unique social class, stood atop this pyramid of social controls. Extravagance among the general population may have been curbed, but the imperial person and his family could still be indulged in any way their advisors might rationalize. Many excavated tombs seem to show that imperial gifts and indulgences allowed at least some persons to be buried in ways that transcended a strict interpretation of applicable sumptuary requirements. These violations, often within the precincts of an imperial necropolis, have provided some of the most striking examples of mural painting and ceramic tomb figurines.

Spirit path at Qianling

Eighteen Imperial Tombs

Stretching across about 100 km (six modern counties) in a fan-shaped arc northwest of modern Xi'an, the Eighteen Imperial Tombs (Shiba Ling) can be understood as the culmination of a long development predating even the Qin First Emperor (Ch. 9). High officials advising the Tang rulers paid considerable attention to the traditions of Qin and especially Han, and evoked those models as part of an overall strategy to justify the dynasty. Reviving the name of the Western Han capital for the Tang city was merely one example of a nod to the past. The Sui and Tang rulers were forced to site their burials on the second-level terrace north of the Wei River, the first level having been coopted by Qin and Han palaces and Han tombs (Ch. 10). Fourteen of the Tang imperial tombs actually utilized the mountains to the north so that individual peaks could serve as mounds. Only four Tang emperor's tombs were built on the flat with man-made earthen mounds. Both plans had Han precedents, although only one Han emperor made a mountain his tomb (the Baling of Emperor Wen, d. 157 BCE). The four Tang tumuli stand at elevations of 500 to 800 m above sea level. The Tang mountain tombs are at elevations between 1200 and 1500 m. All were sited facing south with plans that emphasize axial symmetry along a processional approach advancing toward the north. This orientation contrasts with the Han custom of approaching from the east.

The tomb precincts in fact rework the design of Chang'an. Thus the burial mound or mountain peak surrounded by its own walls corresponds to the Palace City of the capital, so that the emperor's residence in death as in life is the heart of the site within multiple walls. The area of the "spirit path" leading to that innermost zone is comparable, in turn, to the Imperial

City, where ministers and officials who served the emperor were at his beck-and-call. So too in death, albeit with figures frozen in stone. Finally, the larger walled area surrounding the former two zones on three sides corresponds to the residential wards of Chang'an where the elites and general populace lived. At the Tang tombs, this area is given over to satellite burials, most on the south and southeast. (Yet another link and contrast with Han tombs, where satellite burials were placed to the east and northeast.)

Both the Zhaoling and Qianling had walled "palace" compounds draped around a peak serving as

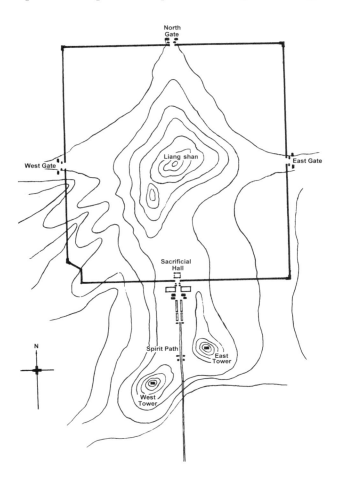

Plan of Qianling

their burial mound. The terrain of the Zhaoling (surrounding Mount Jiujun, elevation 1188 m) is rugged, so flat areas on which to build structures were sculpted from ridges on both its north and south slopes. On the south, the front side, an offering hall was built inside the gate, its foundation 40 m square. Although details have not been reported, an acroterion—the fishtail ceramic fixture that anchors the end of the roof ridge—1.5 m tall was excavated on the spot, an index to the building's scale. Rock-cut chambers with stone walls and vaulted ceilings were also installed on three sides of the peak. One chamber on the east slope was 8 by 2 by 2 m and held large quantities of ceramic figurines and other furnishings. The role of the others remains uncertain. On the north slope, the back side, a suite of gates and galleries ascended step-like terraces. Here in facing galleries were the emperor's famed "Six Chargers," stone reliefs of his favorite steeds (now divided between the Beilin, Xi'an, and the University of Pennsylvania Museum, Philadelphia). To this Gaozong added stone standing figures of fourteen emissaries from the Western Regions.

The plan of the Qianling had much in common. Here the peak, Liangshan, was lower (elevation 1046 m) with gentler slopes, especially those rising from the south. Walls 1.5 km square enclosed the "palace" precinct, with gates at the center of each side and four corner towers which survive to heights of 5 to 10 m. The offering hall on the south was flanked by pavilions, but has not been excavated. Like the north gate of the Zhaoling, the south gate of Qianling was the setting for an array of structures and images. This array begins with two colossal steles 20 m south of the gate: on the east, the "stele without an inscription" stands

7.5 m high, while 60 m distant on the west is an inscription composed by the Empress Wu herself and written by Emperor Zhongzong (their son) commemorating the deceased emperor. It is 7 m tall and a square almost 2 m on a side. Behind the twin steles stand sixty-one life-sized figures (perhaps originally sixty-four) representing emissaries from the Western Regions. At both tombs the gates were fronted by pairs of stone kneeling lions. Those at the Qianling are nearly 3 m in height. (A standing lion from Zhaoling, missing part of its head but with a groom, is on display at the Beilin, Xi'an.)

Only the Qianling retains a full complement of images along the processional approach from the south. The assortment of types found here became the model for subsequent Tang imperial tombs, although later examples were reduced in scale. The ensemble begins with a pair of monolithic, eight-sided stone pillars, 7.5 m tall, separated by the width of the path, 25 m. About 30 m north are a pair of winged horses on stone bases; they measure 3.5 m in height and length. Further north are a pair of slabs with birds (ostriches?) carved in high relief. After these preliminaries, the remainder of the carvings are laid out at 18 m intervals: five pairs of horses and grooms, and ten pairs of standing officials. Each steed differs in appearance, and they, like the Six Chargers of Taizong, may correspond to individual horses in the imperial stud. The frozen, standing officials range in height from 3 to 4.5 m; they wear identical dress. This complement of figures in attendance was modified by subsequent dynasties, but many elements nonetheless survive, as can be seen at the Song tombs (Gongyi, Henan) and in the Ming valley (Ch. 24).

Detail of head of official

Winged horse

Satellite Tombs

About two dozen of the largest sub-imperial tombs have been excavated. The best known are a threesome at Qianling, each the reburial of an imperial prince or princess who died after persecution by Empress Wu. The tomb of Prince Yide (Li Chongrun, d. 706) is described in his epitaph as "like an imperial tomb;" it measures 100 m in length from entrance ramp to rear wall. The tombs of Prince Zhanghuai (Li Xian, d. 684) and Princess Yongtai (Li Xianhui, d. 701) were similar in plan but smaller. This plan derives from sixth-century innovations under the Northern Dynasties as standardized and regulated by Tang sumptuary norms. Each tomb consists of: (1) a sloping ramp, (2) paired wall niches, from two to eight in number where vertical shafts ("sky-wells") brought light and air down from above, and (3) a level corridor leading to the vaulted chamber or chambers. In the three imperial siblings' tombs, the second chamber was outfitted with (4) a sarcophagus carved from stone slabs in imitation of a miniature, tile-roofed wooden hall. Professor Su Bai of Beijing University has suggested that an imperial tomb would have had all of these features (and perhaps more niches) as well as a third chamber.

These two imperial necropolises, and the satellite burials at Qianling in particular, convey a good sense

Sarcophagus from tomb at Li Xian

Wall paintings in tomb of Xincheng Princess

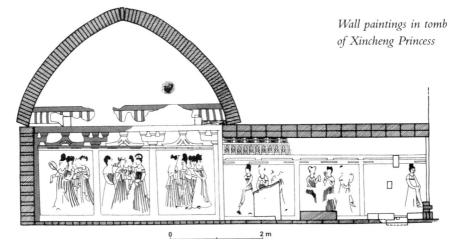

0   2 m

of the standard design established for the Tang emperors. The Zhaoling Museum has a fine display of steles gathered from satellite burials. Both museums display outstanding examples of furnishings created for imperial burials, especially their ceramic figurines. The Shaanxi History Museum also displays excellent figurines from these tombs, but its collection of murals peeled from the walls of various tombs is generally not on display. A special exhibition of this material should not be missed.

Since Luoyang served as the "Eastern Capital" of the Tang, it too is rich in elite burials of that era. The Luoyang City Museum has ample displays, especially of figurines, including a gallery with objects taken from the Gongling in nearby Yanshi, the burial of a son of Gaozong and the Empress Wu from the seventh century. Another important source for Tang tombs is the Astana cemetery near the abandoned Gaochang city site in Turpan and the regional museum there (Ch. 16).

SUGGESTED
READING

A good introduction to Tang imperial ritual is Howard Wechsler, *Offerings of Jade and Silk: Ritual and Symbol in the Legitimation of the T'ang Dynasty* (1985). Ann Paludan, *The Chinese Spirit Road: The Classical Tradition of Stone Tomb Statuary* (1991) devotes a lengthy section to photographs of the many Tang imperial tombs. On tomb figurines, see Virginia L. Bower, *From Court to Caravan: Tomb Sculpture from the Collection of Anthony M. Solomon* (2002); also the catalogue *The Quest for Eternity* (1987) for excavated objects.

Famen Si: A True Relic of the Buddha

19

FAMEN SI MUSEUM
FUFENG, WEST OF XI'AN, SHAANXI
TANG PERIOD, 618–906

Opening pagoda foundations became almost a fad in the 1980s and 90s, leading to criticism by some archaeologists that these excavations were little more than treasure hunting. Deposits within the foundation or fabric of a pagoda often incorporated valuables and rarities, not unlike a tomb. Each pagoda is in principle a repository for a relic (*sarira*): that is, a physical trace of the Buddha, or an object associated with him or some other revered personage or holy site. According to tradition, after the death of Sakyamuni (the Historical Buddha, c. 480 or 400 BCE), his cremated remains were divided among eight burial mounds (stupas), a custom characteristic of Indo–European royalty. Later the great Indian ruler Asoka (a contemporary of the Qin First Emperor) divided these relics into 84,000 pieces, and had them distributed across the Buddhist world, even to China. Each Buddhist stupa or pagoda, its Chinese counterpart, serves as the focus of devotions, usually circumambulation (*pradakshina,* walking in the direction of the sun). Relics are normally housed in special containers (reliquaries), and their burial was often the impetus for pious donations, deluxe objects in the case of well-to-do patrons. Most Chinese temples of any size or consequence should have pagodas with relics, and such finds have been a regular byproduct of archaeological work in China since the 1950s.

Rebuilt pagoda

Famen Si (Dharma Gate Temple) has flourished in the western part of *guanzhong,* about 110 km from Xi'an, since the Northern Dynasties. In summer 1981, heavy rains fell in this area, causing the partial collapse of the temple's Ming-era, brick pagoda. As a protected site on the provincial register, the authorities took responsibility, and in 1987 they began to tear down standing parts of brick structure and clear away rubble. Between February and April they also probed the site, and identified the outlines of several super-imposed foundations. A square earthen block had been the initial, probably Wei-period foundation for a small structure that held a reliquary at its center. This block was surrounded by the much larger footprint of another square structure (26 m on a side), with a perimeter of stone blocks serving as bases for columns. A long passage on the south leading from ground level to the heart of the Wei-period block was also associated with this Tang reconstruction. The passage was reached by a flight of stairs and was sub-divided into four stone chambers separated by doors (a crypt). The Ming pagoda of 20 m diameter had been built on this same plot between 1579 and 1609, with circular footings smaller than the Tang structure but larger than the original Wei block. The contents of the crypt were cleared in May and June, with the last reliquary opened on the eighth day of the fourth lunar month, the traditional date of the Buddha's birth. This lengthy excavation was followed in time by the reconstruction of a new brick pagoda on the original site. The bulk of the deposits, however, were transferred to the new Famen Si Museum next door. Only a single relic was re-interred in the crypt of the newly-built pagoda.

The Crypt and Its Contents

The four sections contained a wealth of objects associated with four different relics, and they had not been disturbed since the 870s when a rich donation was made by the Tang emperors Yizong and Xizong. Thus these deposits provide an extraordinary glimpse into the material culture of Buddhism and the Tang imperial court, through objects of a size and quality literally never seen before. The imperial donation was described in a long text engraved on a stone slab found blocking the door leading to the front chamber. The text not only supplies the date and circumstances of the gift, but also inventories the valuables. Many artifacts found within the crypt match the details in this inventory, indicating, for example, that much of the silver came from the imperial workshops, the Wensi Yuan.

The relics were placed in four separate locations. The front chamber held a miniature stone "King Asoka" stupa housing a bronze model of a timber-frame pagoda. It and its miniature silver coffin are dated to the late seventh century. The central chamber held an even larger stone coffer carved as a canopy with elaborate valances and hangings. Here the relic

Section of the "Underground Palace"

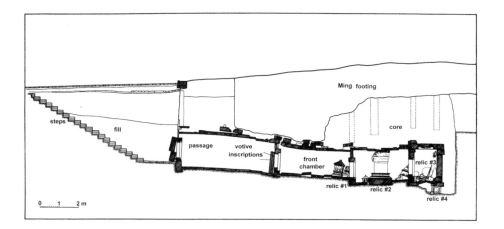

was accompanied by objects dedicated by Emperor Zhongzong in 708. The rear chamber was packed with offerings: large silver censers, lotus leaves, altar fittings, as well as tea utensils of the highest quality. The third relic found here was housed in eight nested boxes dated 871 dedicated by Emperors Yizong and Xizong. A fourth relic was discovered in a niche under the floor of the rear chamber only after that area was emptied. Also within multiple boxes and nested jade and crystal coffins, these objects are dated to the "full Tang period," the early eighth century.

Why Four Relics?

Famen Si was renowned as the resting place of "an authentic body relic of the Buddha," by tradition one of four Buddha relics to come to China in the middle ages. (The other three temples and their relics have not survived.) The intense public veneration and lavish imperial patronage this relic evoked are well documented in historical records. On at least six occasions, the Famen Si relic was removed from its resting place at the temple and presented to the court and capital as the focus of both public and imperial devotions. In 660–662, the relic was taken to Luoyang; the stone King Asoka stupa in the front chamber may date from that event. Again in 704–708, the relic was sent to the Eastern Capital for the Empress Wu; the stone coffer in the shape of a canopy in the middle chamber was created on that occasion. In 760, 790, 819, and 871–74, the relic came to Chang'an and was admitted to the palace. The 819 event prompted the court official Han Yu to memorialize against what he regarded as outrageous conduct, writing: "How then, when he has long been dead, could his rotten bones, the foul and unlucky remains of his body, be rightly

Diagram of objects found
in the rear chamber

admitted to the palace?" The final celebration in 871–74 apparently led to refurbishing the pagoda and its crypt, and to the extraordinary riches found in the rear chamber in 1987.

The recovery of four separate relics, none of them a human finger bone as tradition claims, raises several questions. Was one of these relics regarded as the primary one, perhaps that in the eight boxes prepared in 871–74 for the rear chamber? If so, were the three other relics regarded as replicas or otherwise of lesser status? And if the most important relic occupied the rear chamber, then what do we make of the hidden deposit in the floor? Could these be three additional relics gathered together during the Tang period, perhaps during or after the persecution of the 840s engineered by the imperial court? While the housings for all of these relics seem to have been created for a "true body relic," several of them show signs of wear that could testify to their extraction from this or other crypts. The two stone coffers in the front and middle chambers do not fit well in those spaces (and hence originally were installed in a chamber of different size and shape?), and show the most damage. Both, however, would be sensible if designed for a simpler, square reliquary chamber, the kind standard in the early and middle Tang periods. Indeed the multi-chamber crypt at Famen Si, so far a unique example, may have been constructed for the first time in the middle Tang by an imperial patron.

Indeed, the crypt and its reliquaries testify to several adaptations of Indian Buddhism to Chinese customs. The oldest reliquaries known in East Asia are square stone coffers with lids, housing multiple containers. These coffers were placed in the foundation and could not be reopened without disassembling the pagoda above. By the late sixth century, probably under imperial Sui patronage, reliquaries first took the shape of miniature coffins, usually in silver. At the same time the lid of the stone coffer with its inscription mimics the shape and decoration of an epitaph cover. The stone coffers in the shape of stupas and canopies, and the bronze model found within one, are themselves examples of the adaptation of Indian stupas to Chinese architectural style. Indeed, the bronze model may reflect the appearance of the early Tang pagoda built at Famen Si. By the middle or late Tang, perhaps even as early as Empress Wu, however, the Famen Si crypt was made more like a tomb. The series of stone chambers accessible by stairs and divided by doorways closely parallels the plan of an elite burial. Doorways with engraved panels, jambs, and lintels imitate typical tomb decor. This new structure was well adapted to the desire to remove and display the relic at intervals.

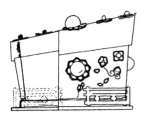

Miniature silver coffins

The lavish donations of the 870s may be explained in part as an effort by the court and its Buddhist supporters to atone for the major proscription and persecution of Buddhism that devastated the Tang realm in the 840s. Thousands of Buddhist monks and nuns were returned to lay status. Temples with their precious relics, images, and wall paintings were destroyed. Only four temples were allowed to remain open in the capital (Ci'en Si, home of the Great Goose pagoda, being one). The esoteric images of the Anguo Si found buried in a deep well on site, and the dozens of small, gilt images found at Ximing Si, were probably also by-products of this persecution. Indeed, little of Tang Buddhist architecture, excepting stone and masonry pagodas, predates this event. One small wooden hall on Mount Wutai dated to the 750s is the only certain exception to this rule known at present.

Donations from Emperor Yizong featured not only deluxe examples in gold and silver such as a monk's staff, "begging" bowls, censers, altar fittings, serving vessels, and tea utensils, but also rare items from distant cultures. Several kinds of glass are represented, including Islamic blue saucers and a bottle from the eastern Mediterranean of Roman or Byzantine date. The inventory text also names some of the celadon in the crypt as *mi se* ("secret color formula") ware, a highly-prized stoneware from southeastern China whose actual identity has been disputed among ceramics specialists. The imperial gifts even included pieces of miniature clothing decorated with gold-stitch embroidery thought to be from the hand of the Empress Wu. The material culture of the Famen Si crypt is thus a corollary to the luxury life style evoked in Tang poetry or pictured in murals at Dunhuang.

Islamic glass

Kneeling Bodhisattva

Buddhist archaeology has become an increasingly rich vein. A considerable number of pagodas have yielded treasures in recent years, among them the Ruiguang Si Pagoda (Suzhou, Jiangsu), and the Jingzhi Si crypt (Dingzhou, Hebei), both of early Song date. More recently the Leifeng Pagoda (Hangzhou, Zhejiang; Ch. 22), was found to contain a wealth of objects including one of the finest King Asoka stupa reliquaries.

SUGGESTED
READING

Famen Si awaits a worthy survey in English. Two short articles by Roderick Whitfield introduce the finds: "The Significance of the Famensi Deposit," *Orientations* 5 (1990): 84–85, and his entry in Yang, *The Golden Age of Chinese Archaeology* (1999), pp. 462–85. Han Yu's "Memorial on the Bone of the Buddha" is translated in W. T. de Bary and I. Bloom, *Sources of Chinese Tradition,* (1999), vol. 1, pp. 583–85.

Mogao: Caves of the Thousand Buddhas

20

DUNHUANG, GANSU
NORTHERN DYNASTIES–YUAN, 4TH–14TH C.
WORLD HERITAGE SITE

Dunhuang has been a gateway in both ancient and modern times. During the Han and Tang periods, this oasis at the far western end of the Gansu corridor was the jumping off point for travel both north and south of the Takla Makan desert, the routes later immortalized in von Richthofen's phrase "the Silk Roads." Han defensive walls extended past the oasis to end at two checkpoints: Yumen Guan and Yang Guan, where ruins survive today. Han cavalry expeditions to the Western Regions came and went by this route. In the Tang, Dunhuang became Shazhou, "Sand Prefecture," a flourishing entrepot and way station between points west—the states of Turpan (Ch. 16, Jiaohe), Qiuci (Kucha), Khotan, and beyond—and Chang'an's Western Market (Ch. 17). The cave-chapels and temples that grew up here from the fourth century gained the patronage of local elites as well as an international community. The murals, sculpted images, and silk paintings from the "Caves of the Thousand Buddhas" provide stunning, full-color snapshots of this cosmopolitan age.

View of cliff face, Mogao

At the turn of the twentieth century, these caves and especially manuscripts and paintings recovered from them brought Dunhuang to the world's attention. A brilliant culture from the past was evoked through words and images "rescued" by the exploits of such redoubtable explorers as Mark Aurel Stein (1862–1943) and Paul Pelliot (1878–1945). Their legacy lives on in museum collections in London, Paris, and elsewhere. Even so, few experiences in China match a visit to the Mogao cliff and its chapels, where a vivid, firsthand encounter with the past awaits.

Cave-chapels (or grottoes, *shi ku si*) are ubiquitous in North and Northwest China. Although they differ in particulars of setting and scale, they have in common a one-time community of Buddhist monks who established a secluded retreat. Such a retreat should be far enough from population centers to allow meditation and other religious practice without undue disruption, but close enough to travel routes and towns to make lay patronage feasible. Seasonal retreats were part of the life of the Historical Buddha and his disciples, who interrupted their mendicant life style during the monsoon. Permanent rock-cut complexes, with caves for worship (*caitya*) and residence (*vihara*), appeared in greater India and Central Asia long before they developed in China Proper. In addition to Dunhuang, cave-chapels were created at many sites further east along the Gansu corridor (Maijishan, Bingling Si), and near the imperial capitals of the Northern Dynasties (Yungang at Datong, Longmen at Luoyang).

The natural cliff face outside the Dunhuang oasis is a friable conglomerate with pebbles in a matrix of sandy soil. While suitable for excavating chapels, the material resisted sculpture; as a result the images here are clay modeled on wooden armatures. On the other hand, the cliff face encouraged mural decoration, painting in ink and color on a dry plaster ground (not fresco). The magnificent preservation of so much painting distinguishes Dunhuang from most sites in China. Yungang and Longmen today are utterly devoid of early painted surfaces, although some images repainted in recent times will be seen. While other sites in Xinjiang, like Bezeklik (north of Turpan), Kizil, and Kumtura (both outside Kucha) also boast extensive murals, they unfortunately are less

The Mogao Chapels

well-preserved. The limitations of other major sites make the Mogao "Caves of the Thousand Buddhas" even more impressive.

According to a text found in cave no. 156, activity at the Mogao cliff face may date as early as the third century. The oasis had become a center for translation of Buddhist sutras by this time. Two fourth-century dates are given for the first cave-chapels: a tenth-century text recovered by Pelliot suggests 352–53, while other sources state that in 366 a monk named Yuezun saw a "golden radiance and one thousand Buddhas" while in meditation, perhaps a reference to the sunset glow on hills opposite the cliff. In any case, the traveling monk Faxian, the first Chinese Buddhist to visit North India, stopped briefly in 400, and the cave site is also mentioned in the "Treatise on Buddhism and Daoism" in the Northern Wei history. The oldest surviving caves (nos. 268, 272, 275), however, are dated by style to the 420s, the Northern Liang period. From these humble beginnings, the site grew steadily. A total of 37 chapels predate the Sui; 79 are extant from the Sui period, 232 from the Tang, 27 from the tenth century, 34 from early Song, and 64 from the Xi Xia (Tangut) occupation of the 11th–13th centuries. The main cliff face has more than 490 chapels, while several hundred empty caves are to be found to the north. They may have been hermitages for monks and housed artisans employed at the site.

The chapels served several purposes, as their plans suggest. In the fifth and sixth centuries, the most important type was a "stupa-pillar" plan: a pillar connecting floor to ceiling was carved from the cliff with a passage for circumambulation on three sides. A chamber inside the door across the axis provided space

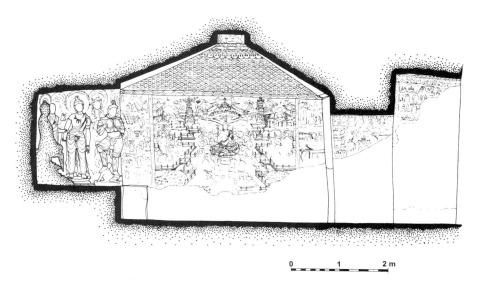

for communal worship before the pillar. Most examples have a pitched ceiling running from side to side,
and niches both under its gable and on the four sides
of the pillar. This plan is also seen in early chapels at
Kizil. The most long-lasting plan at Mogao was a
"canopy roof" type, with a four-slope ceiling rising to
a recessed central coffer; this created a large common
space for worship, complemented by an altar niche in
the rear wall. The painted ceiling might evoke the decoration of a free-standing Buddha hall, while the large
wall areas were appropriate for ensembles of painted
images. An example like cave no. 220 (dated 642) displays a selection of Pure Lands on the walls flanking
the rear pentad with the Buddha of the West,
Amitabha. A later development of this plan has a raised
altar platform, with screens behind the sculpted
images, and room for circumambulation.

Several less common plans are also found at
Mogao. Two caves feature colossal Buddhas (cave no.
96, at 33 m, dated 695, and no. 130, at 26 m, dated

*Canopy ceiling plan of
cave no. 45*

eighth century). In each case these Buddhas are high reliefs with multi-level facades fronting them. Such large Buddha images are found at other sites, but rarely are their architectural facades intact. Two other Mogao caves are dedicated to the Parinirvana ("extinction") of the Buddha (no. 148 and no. 158); the former has a reclining image 17 m long against the rear wall.

While hundreds of Buddhist temples and dozens of cave-chapels survive in China, few have the breadth and depth of subject matter, and especially early evidence, that the Mogao chapels offer. Most free-standing temple halls date at the earliest from the Song and Liao periods (10th–12th centuries; Ch. 21). Other early cave-chapel sites generally display a more restricted range of subjects and only rarely any pictorial art. The early chapels at Mogao, by contrast, are rich in imagery of the Buddha of the Future, Maitreya, while later examples reflect the rise of devotion to the Buddha of the Western Pure Land, Amitabha, and its principal attendant, Guanyin (Avalokitesvara). The Tang caves in particular transcribe the development of Western Pure Land imagery, with ever more detailed depictions of that realm, as well as other Pure Lands. Narratives from the *Lotus Sutra* and from texts promoting meditation on Amitabha also appear. The later Tang cults of Guanyin in its many manifestations, and of Dizang (Ksitigarbha) fill many walls. By the tenth century, guardian kings, royal donors from Khotan and elsewhere, topographic views of Mount Wutai, the stories of Sariputra, and other teaching tales are on display, often side-by-side in the largest chapels. Unlike Yungang or Longmen, where fine carving stone permitted endless dedications of small devotional images and niches, at Mogao the caves were generally designed and executed at one time, although later repainting sometimes made over entire walls or ceilings. And unlike the unpainted sandstone or limestone of most sites in China Proper, the walls at Dunhuang are filled with color, fine painted details, and cartouches labeling images and naming donors.

The Sutra Cave

The "Sutra Cave" or "Library Cave" is now designated as cave no. 17 by the Dunhuang Academy. It is a small excavation on the north side of the entrance to the much grander cave no. 16. No. 17 was an image hall dedicated to an important late Tang prelate named Hongbian (died 860s), whose portrait image, now re-installed, is the oldest in Chinese art history. The doorway to no. 17 was walled over some time in the eleventh century when it was filled with thousands of worn-out sutras, documents, banners, and other materials gathered from the many temples at the oasis. No convincing explanation for the creation of this cache has been offered. (The coming of the Tangut Xi Xia

Hongbian image chapel ("Sutra Cave")

was once suggested, but they were Buddhists and became major patrons of the chapels, hardly a threat.) The discovery of this cache is now dated to June of 1900, when Wang Yuanlu, a self-appointed caretaker and Daoist priest, first opened the deposit. By cajolery and donations, Aurel Stein and later Paul Pelliot managed to make off with thousands of Wang's finds. Stein's scrolls and paintings were selected by Wang, and date from the fifth to the tenth centuries. Their cataloguer, Lionel Giles, once noted that most of Stein's 8100 items were Buddhist, with multitudinous copies of popular sutras, for example over 1000 texts of the *Lotus Sutra*. Pelliot (who unlike Stein knew Chinese) made his own selection, and claimed to have acquired a more varied and hence valuable assortment. Stein's material was later divided between the British Museum, London, and the National Museum in New Delhi. Pelliot's library went to the Bibliothèque National and Musée Guimet. This episode in the history of the site is told in a special display hall opposite cave no. 17.

Cave-chapel Archaeology

Until the 1950s, most cave-chapel sites in China were given little protection and had been studied mostly by non-Chinese scholars. Since that time cave-chapel archaeology has developed into a vibrant field that merges archaeological methods (excavation, typological classification) with art historical and Buddhological analysis. The sites are not only important architectural complexes and artistic achievements; they also record through their inscriptions and images many aspects of medieval Buddhism and society. All of the cave-chapel sites are listed on national or provincial registers, and restorations have gone forward in almost every case.

*Cave no. 53 facade
rendering by Xiao Mo*

These range from stabilizing cliffs to installing new walkways and doors as protection from the elements and visitors. A number of excavations have also taken place. At Dunhuang and Yungang, for example, digs at the foot of the cliff face uncovered the foundations of lost timber structures. Also at Dunhuang, systematic clearing of the northern caves recovered artifacts including artisans' paraphernalia. Careful study of cave plans, decoration, and style juxtaposed with documentary evidence has created more precise dating for many sites, with many implications for the history of Buddhism and Buddhist arts in China.

In addition to Yungang and Longmen, the many cave-chapels of Xinjiang and Gansu are highly recommended. The sites are invariably attractive, even if remote and reachable only after a bumpy ride or long hike. Bingling Si (now on a Yellow River reservoir outside Lanzhou, Gansu) has a colossal cliff-face Buddha, as well as dozens of niches from the Wei and Tang periods. A natural grotto above the colossus boasts the oldest dated images in China, c. 420. Kizil and Kumtura are sited amid desolate locations, reminiscent of Utah canyon lands, outside Kucha. Both are open for the more adventuresome visitor. Other less typical sites are also worthwhile: Dazu (outside of Chongqing), with fascinating reliefs from the Song period, and Feilaifeng (outside Hangzhou), with Tibetan-Buddhist subject matter from the Yuan period.

SUGGESTED READING
Roderick Whitfield, Susan Whitfield, and Neville Agnew, *Cave Temples of Mogao* (2000) is the best concise overview of the site, with excellent color photography of murals and images. For accounts of European explorers, see Peter Hopkirk's lively *Foreign Devils on the Silk Road* (1980), and Jeannette Mirsky, *Sir Mark Aurel Stein: Archaeological Exlorer* (1977), which quotes extensively from Stein's letters and reports. Arthur Waley, *Ballads and Stories from Tun-huang* (1960), translates popular literature recovered from the library cave. Roderick Whitfield and Anne Farrer, *The Caves of the Thousand Buddhas* (1990) is a catalogue that introduces the Stein collections in the British Museum, London; so too does Susan Whitfield's *The Silk Road: Trade, Travel, War and Faith* (2004), sponsored by the British Library to celebrate Stein's centenary. The International Dunhuang Project's website is also informative: http://idp.bl.uk.

Song, Yuan, and Ming
(960–1644)

One of the most durable myths associated with China was a vision of the "Celestial Kingdom" as an unchanging society, its institutions created by the Confucian sages of antiquity and perpetuated by enlightened scholar-bureaucrats. European Catholic missionaries, some of whom diligently studied Chinese language and culture in the late Ming and early Qing, helped create this myth in their writings, the first serious works to introduce China to Europe. A good part of what they conveyed was what they were taught by Chinese scholars, who for ideological purposes had created their own myths. The earliest histories of China written in European languages thus convey a view of imperial history crafted by Song and later scholars. Modern historical scholarship has made great strides in undoing these myths and recreating the realities of later Chinese history. Here too archaeology plays a creative role.

The two Song regimes, founded by a general in the tenth-century, ruled from 960–1279. The Northern Song (960–1126) was centered on the North China plain at modern Kaifeng (Henan), known then as Bianliang or the Eastern Capital. This was an historic shift in the position of the national capital, ending the long-lasting Chang'an period (Ch. 17). After myriad floods of the Yellow River, Song remains at Kaifeng are many meters below modern ground level. The Southern Song (1127–1279) is bracketed by two traumatic events: the fall of Bianliang to the Ruzhen (dynastic title: Jin, 1115–1234), which sent the court south across the Yangzi (hence the designation "southern"), and the final demise of the imperial court at the hands of the Mongols (dynastic title: Yuan, 1260–1368). The temporary capital of the Song at modern Hangzhou (Zhejiang) is slowly emerging from underneath the overlay of the more recent occupations of the city (Ch. 22).

The fate of Song obviously was intertwined with the conquest states of its northern frontier: Liao (916–1125), Xi Xia (1038–1227), Jin, and Yuan. They have in common non-Han ethnicities (Qidan, Tangut, Ruzhen, Mongol), lifestyles that made the transition from steppe mobility to sedentary city-dwelling, and the pervasive adoption of Chinese institutions and customs that allowed them to create hybrid states powerful enough to overrun the north, or in the case of the Mongols, the whole of East Asia. The Mongols have been the best known to Europeans, due to their threat to Russia and Eastern Europe in the thirteenth century, and to early accounts such as Marco Polo. The city that Polo described, Cambaluc ("the Khan's city"), lies under modern Beijing, and has been reclaimed in pieces via excavations (Ch. 23).

Like Song, the Ming (1368–1644) was an ethnic-Han dynasty, its founder, Zhu Yuanzhang, a commoner like Liu Bang of the Han. Evicting the Mongols in 1368 did not end their threat. The frontier remained dangerous, and the third Ming emperor, Zhu Di better known as Yongle, built his new capital atop the Mongol-Yuan city in part as a staging area for campaigns he led from the saddle against the Mongols. (His tomb also began development of the Ming Valley; Ch. 24.) The northward shift of the capital, first by the Mongols and then Yongle, inaugurates a Peking period in Chinese history that continues today. But then as now, the population and economic centers of the later empires were further south, especially the Lower Yangzi macroregion epitomized by such cities as Nanjing, Suzhou, and most recently Shanghai.

Historical writings are abundant for the later empires, starting with *The Cambridge History of China* (vols. 5–8 for Song through Ming). Two single-volume works can also be recommended: Jacques Gernet, *A History of Chinese Civilization* (1982), and Frederick W. Mote, *Imperial China: 900–1800* (1999).

SUGGESTED READING

21 Timber-frame Structures of Song and Liao

TIANJIN; TAIYUAN AND YINGXIAN, SHANXI
SONG AND LIAO, 10TH–11TH CENTURIES

In pre-modern times, the notional category architecture was approximated by the term *tu mu* ("earth and wood"). This pairing acknowledges the components of most buildings of all functional types and status. Earth—raw soil—was the building material of cave dwellings and most graves, the stuff of pounded earth foundations, as well as the makings of adobe and of fired brick, tile, and other architectural pottery. The use of earth and wood can be traced from the Neolithic forward step by step. Baked brick and tile became prominent by the early Imperial period for roofs and paving, and for the fabric of tomb chambers. At the same time, wooden timbers became more important as the structural frame of buildings large and small.

But the durability of masonry and timber-frame structures differs considerably. Leaving aside Han stone gate towers, most at tomb sites in Henan, Shandong, and Sichuan, the oldest surviving examples of the former are Buddhist pagodas from the sixth and seventh centuries. The oldest, the Mount Song Pagoda (Dengfeng, Henan, c. 520–24), a project of the Northern Wei court, has long outlived its timber and earth counterpart, the Yongning Si Pagoda at Luoyang

(Ch. 13). By contrast, the earliest extant timber structure is the Main Hall of Nanchan Si (c. 782) on Mount Wutai, Shanxi, in its day an insignificant temple and a lucky survivor of the persecution of Buddhism in the ninth century. The more famous East Main Hall of Foguang Si, c. 857, also on Wutai, is the only large timber structure that predates the tenth century. Thus, almost nothing of timber-frame construction prior to late Tang remains, although documentary evidence testifies to its dominance. Shanxi province, especially its hard to reach corners, is a veritable museum of ancient timber buildings of every kind (halls, towers, stages) dating from the tenth to the thirteenth century, as well as later. At least seventy of the 106 oldest structures known today in all of China still stand there.

Guanyin Pavilion, Dule Si, Tianjin

Timber Construction by Modules

By the early imperial era, timber frames could carry the weight of roofs without the assistance of load-bearing, solid walls. Even though no timber structures from Qin and Han survive (other than wooden burial chambers), we know that squared posts and tie beams for the frame and interlocking blocks and arms (*dou gong*) for bracket clusters had emerged. Buddhist cave-chapel reliefs offer evidence for the elaboration of this timber-frame system prior to Tang. The system reached its first plateau of sophisticated design in the Sui and Tang.

Wood was reasonably abundant in early times, if less so later, and readily worked with the iron and steel tools available. Wood has great tensile strength, so that framing a space with posts and lintels and spanning a roof using tie-beams and truss was efficient in terms of the quantity and size of the material required. Assembly and repairs were convenient because carpenters avoided rigid joinery in favor of tenons and mortises. These structures therefore resisted earthquakes, since the frame was flexible. The system created between Han and Tang allowed buildings to be constructed from parts made to a common module, usually the width and height of a bracket arm (*gong*).

The earliest written demonstration of this system appeared late in Northern Song, the justly famous *Ying zao fa shi* (*Building Standards*, c. 1103) attributed to Li Jie, an imperial official. The guidelines posit a standard unit or module: the height of a bracket arm rendered in any of eight grades. Each building project, such as main hall with subordinate structures like gates and galleries, was assigned a grade from 1 to 8 based on its importance and position in the ensemble. The hall was built at a higher grade, while the galleries and gates will be lower by several steps. Measurements in inches derived from the module were pre-determined for each grade. Every timber was then manufactured in quantity following those dimensions, some larger, some smaller, probably from rulers that master carpenters carried. The module determined such basic features as the height and diameter of columns, the spacing of bays (adjacent columns), the placement of bracket sets on lintels, and the roof rise and pitch. Building any structure was largely a matter of manufacturing enough of all components—columns, beams, blocks, and arms—to fulfill the requirements of the building.

Structural Principles

The timber-frame buildings introduced here embody common structural principles. Each building can be divided into three tiers: foundation with column grid, bracket clusters, and roof frame.

A foundation usually consists of: (1) a mass of pounded earth that supports floor and surrounding porch or gallery, and (2) large stone blocks set in the earth to carry the columns. The top surface is generally covered with ceramic tile and usually faced with dressed stone. Balustrades, ramps, and steps may also be stone. An abandoned building may well be stripped of its stone balustrades and floor tiles, while heavy stone column bases were usually left in place.

Columns rest on stone bases without attachment. Dead weight held them in place, but they could shift in response to a strong tremor. The height of a column and the span between adjacent columns are generally equal. In Tang times these dimensions reached as much as 5 m, later as much as 7 m. Columns are spaced at variable intervals: the central bay widest, flanking bays reduced slightly, and the terminal (outer-most) bays generally smaller still. Likewise the first and last bays in depth are generally shallow, while the central bay is generally deeper. Most buildings are an odd number of bays across their front and rear facades, and an even number of bays in depth as seen from the sides. By the Song period, if not before, columns were given features to enhance the appearance of stability and grace. Thus the columns arrayed across the facade become slightly taller as they move out from the central bay (called "rise"), and are angled slightly inward from true vertical ("batter"). Around the perimeter, columns are tied together both at their bases (hence the need to step over thresholds) and heads. This of course strengthens the grid, side-to-side and in depth. This sturdy interlocked column grid carries the enormous weight of roof frame and tile, while also allowing the structure to flex.

The column grid allows complete flexibility in the placement of partitions to define interior spaces. Small halls might have only a perimeter circuit of columns with tie-beams that spanned the depth of the building at ceiling level (as at Nanchan Si). In this case, a completely unobstructed interior could be created for the altar and images of this Buddhist hall. Two parallel circuits of columns might be created by subtracting some central columns (as with the third of five rows at Foguang Si). In this scheme, the interior space (called "inner trough") is open and surrounded by an inner circuit of columns; the outer space serves as an ambulatory delimited by the inner circuit and the columns on the exterior. Tenth- and eleventh-century structures play with these options by subtracting columns in one or more rows or by displacing

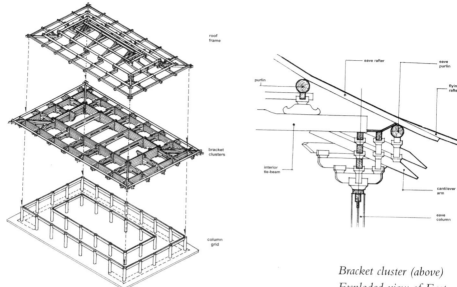

Bracket cluster (above)
Exploded view of East
Main Hall, Foguang Si
(left)

columns from their normal position in each bay. Thus a porch (or gallery) could easily be added to the front of a building by hanging the door and window panels of the front wall one or more rows inward from columns under the eaves.

The most complex structural components are bracket sets or clusters, usually pegged to the top of columns, which transmit the weight of the roof down through the columns to the stone bases. Larger halls (those higher in grade and hence larger in scale) generally also have one or more intermediate bracket sets placed on lintels between columns. In any set, a large block (*dou*) cradles the two lowest level arms (*gong*), which interlock and cross at right angles in slots prepared to receive them. These arms are generally short; they terminate with smaller blocks (with slots in one direction only) that accept the next tier. The lowest level transverse arms (those at right angles to the facade) are actually the ends of the interior tie-beams that cross from one column to the next in depth. Likewise, the lowest level lateral arms (those in line with the facade) may be tie-beams that strengthen the sets side-to-side; these may be carved with the silhouette of an arm. Additional tiers of interlocked arms, and even cantilever arms (called *ang*), elevate interior tie-beams above the column heads and reduce the spans between columns. On the exterior, these multi-tiered sets elevate and project the eaves above and away from the columns. This brings important benefits: in winter months, maximum light and warmth penetrate the interior, while in the heat of summer maximum shade is produced. The cantilevered eaves also protect the bases of columns and surrounding surfaces from the elements.

Roof frames rest on tiers of transverse tie-beams above the column-head bracket sets. If a ceiling is dropped in, the timbers above it are often left rough, while an exposed roof frame will have finished timbers. Superimposed tie-beams mount toward the ridge at each end of the building. An inverted V-strut or a short kingpost at the top usually carries the ridge pole, which runs parallel to the facade. The placement of purlins parallel to the ridge determines the pitch and curvature of a roof. These purlins carry short rafters laid at right angles; they do not run from ridge to eave as one piece. A roof frame therefore has several steps coming down from the ridge, and if their spans and heights are varied, a quite dramatic sweeping curvature is produced. Finally, boards are laid across the rafters. Ceramic roof tile is set on a thick coating of mud; together mud and tile create an enormous load that bears down on the frame, bracket sets, and columns. This has the practical benefit of keeping the roof and building in place against high winds.

Many of the one-hundred-plus buildings that survive from the eighth through twelfth centuries are found in rural and mountainous settings, although some survive amidst bustling towns.

Main Halls. The pre-eminent early example is the East Main Hall of Foguang Si, on Mount Wutai (dated 857) discussed above. Even more impressive is the "Sage Mother" Hall of the Jin Ci (Jin Shrine) in the outskirts of Taiyuan, dated 1023–1032. Part of a major shrine honored by both imperial and local patrons, this building is perhaps as close as one can now come to Song-era palace-style architecture. This hall is seven bays across and six deep, about 26 by 21 m. In contrast to the Foguang Si East Hall with its five rows of parallel columns and inner and outer "troughs," the Sage Mother Hall grid is an exercise in subtracting columns and subdividing the interior to create a varied plan. A single-bay gallery tracks around both sides and the rear, while a porch two bays deep fronts the walled interior, which is five bays by three. By removing four columns in the second row (porch) and eight in the two rows inside the walls, large spaces are opened in what would otherwise be a forest. But the structure above the grid is even more complex, with short columns rising from transverse tie-beams to carry the front eaves over the open porch. Another striking contrast to the Tang hall is the size of bracket sets: at Foguang Si, the several tiers of blocks and arms are half the column height, while at the Sage Mother Hall, they are only 30 percent. Also, while the cantilever-arms at Foguang Si are functional, those at this eleventh-century hall have become ornamental. The hall is further ornamented by dragons entwined around

Building Types

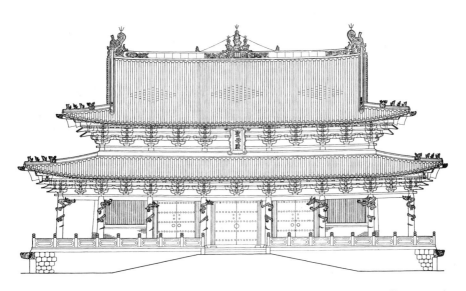

Elevation of Sage Mother Hall, Jin Ci

the columns, and the grace of the roof's sweeping tile work.

Pavilions. Ten structures are found in Shanxi, Hebei, Tianjin, and Liaoning from the period when Qidan people ruled as the Liao dynasty (907–1125). The earliest is the Guanyin Pavilion of Dule Si, a small compound in the heart of Ji County, rural Tianjin, reached either from that city or Beijing. The main gate and pavilion are dated 984, and at the time they were first studied (1931), they were thought to be the oldest extant wooden structures in China.

Although on the exterior the Guanyin Pavilion looks to be two-stories, the interior frame is actually three stacked tiers of columns, following the inner/outer trough scheme of Foguang Si. At five bays across by four deep, the inner trough necessitated subtracting two columns from the central (third) row. By setting shorter columns atop the bracket sets of both the first and second stories, an open well was created for the colossal statue of Guanyin (Avalokitesvara) 16

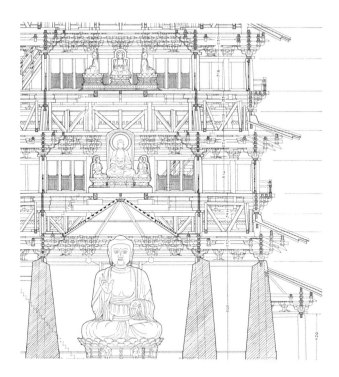

*Section of the
Wooden Pagoda*

m in height. A balcony is carried by the cantlevered bracket arms atop the second tier of columns, while the main roof and skirting lower eave are carried by the sets atop the third and first levels, respectively.

Pagodas. In contrast to hundreds of masonry examples, only one wooden pagoda survives from pre-modern times. It is the great tower at Fogong Si in rural Yingxian, Shanxi, accessible from Datong. This Liao structure is dated 1056, and its survival against the tides of history, earthquakes, lightning, and fire is nothing short of miraculous.

The Wooden Pagoda is eight-sided, the main entry on the south. Two circuits of columns imbedded in thick masonry walls define an inner core and ambulatory; a porch adds a second, exterior ambulatory. The porch adds its eave to the four above and the main roof surmounted by a tall iron spire; the overall height is 67 m. Like the East Main Hall and Guanyin Pavilion, the Wooden Pagoda consists of superimposed tiers: five floor-levels, four mezzanines, and a roof. These tiers actually comprise nineteen structural layers of columns, tie-beams, braces, and bracket sets. Each structural layer is well integrated, so each amounts to an independent structure. Every floor is open at its core, so that five levels with altars and images could be installed for visiting pilgrims.

Suggested Reading

Liang Ssu-ch'eng, *A Pictorial History of Chinese Architecture* (1984) is a presentation using drawings made by Liang (1901–1972), one of the pioneers of the field. Lothar Ledderose, *Ten Thousand Things* (2000) devotes a chapter to the modular system. The more recent Fu Xinian et al, *Chinese Architecture* (2002) gives an overview of the history of architecture with good photographs and excellent maps and plans of capitals and palaces. Nancy Shatzman Steinhardt, *Liao Architecture* (1997), discusses all the buildings mentioned above.

Lin'an: A Celadon Realm

22

HANGZHOU, ZHEJIANG
WU-YUE, 907–978
AND SOUTHERN SONG, 1127–1279

In his *Travels,* Marco Polo (1254–1324) described to Europe the great city of Hangzhou as "without doubt the finest and most splendid city in the world." His assessment of this metropolis, with a population of more than a million squeezed between the Qiantang River on the east and West Lake opposite, correlates reasonably well with even more extensive accounts in Chinese literature. (It also reinforces the credibility of the great Venetian as a reporter of the wonders of the east.) Like Polo, Chinese writers marveled at the quality of life in this beautiful setting, an impression still common among the city's visitors.

The city Polo encountered was known either as *xingzai suo,* the "in-transit resting place" of the emperor, or after 1138, by its official name, Lin'an. The former term specified the city as a mere interruption in the glorious Song, which had temporarily lost control of its proper capital, its emperor, and his heir to the invading Jin armies. In line with the view that the Song armies must shortly re-conquer the north, the imperial house moved into a provincial city of modest scale and attributes. As time wore on temporary imperial tombs were also established further south

View of West Lake   near Shaoxing, to serve until the dynastic necropolis in
Henan could be reclaimed. It is this term that Polo
records as "Quinsai" or "Kinsai." The city had its origins in the Qin-Han era near hills north and west of
the lake. It had been re-established on its present location in the Sui (589–617), the better to serve the
Grand Canal. Only later, in Tang and Northern Song
times, did West Lake take shape through the efforts of
such literati magistrates as Bo Zhuyi and Su Dongpo,
and various hydraulic engineers.

Hangzhou in the Tenth Century

The prefectural city that the itinerant Song court took
over in the twelfth century had been the capital two
centuries earlier of a short-lived kingdom called Wu-
Yue (907–78). Three generations of the Qian dynasty
left their mark by renewing the city walls and building
palaces on high ground near Fenghuang Shan, the
present Zhongshan South Road, which would later
become the Song palace. The Qian rulers patronized

construction of one of the city's great monuments, the
Leifeng Pagoda on a small promontory at the south
end of the lake. Collapsed in 1924, the site was
recently cleared and excavated with the goal of
rebuilding the structure, which had echoed another
famous landmark, the Baochu Pagoda across the water
to the north. The lower levels of the Leifeng Pagoda
were in good condition, and in 2001 a crypt in its base
was opened to reveal a treasure-trove of precious furnishings. Like the Famen Si crypt (Ch. 19), its contents
are objects of the highest quality bestowed by imperial
patrons. The *mi se* celadons of Famen in fact emanated
from Wu-Yue kilns, and have been found at many sites
of this region. When completely rebuilt, the new
eight-sided, five-story brick and timber pagoda will be
72 m tall. The tenth-century court also promoted the
construction of many other pagodas in this area,
including two stone structures at Lingyan Si and the
enormous Liuhe Pagoda on the banks of the Qiantang
River estuary. (The latter displays the history of this
Buddhist architectural type.)

*King Asoka stupa,
Leifeng Pagoda*

The Wu-Yue imperial tombs were sited west of
Hangzhou in hills outside the city. At least four sump-
tuous tombs of imperial rank have been reported, the
mausoleum of Qian Yuanjin (the second ruler, d. 941)
and his consort, Wu Hanyue (d. 952), rather close to
the modern city, and the Kangling of a consort née Ma
(d. 939) some 50 km further west at Lin'an. These lavish burials feature fine carvings and painting (even with
gold), and should be compared with the tomb chambers of Wang Jian (Chengdu) and the Southern Tang
mausoleums outside Nanjing. The Wu-Yue tombs have
also been important sources of early celadon.

Hangzhou in Southern Song

In spite of its historical renown, archaeological exploration of the Southern Song city was delayed until the 1980s, when a Lin'an Excavation Team was formed as a cooperative venture of the Hangzhou City Institute of Cultural Relics and Archaeology, the Zhejiang Institute, and the Institute of Archaeology, Beijing. As the city has modernized over the last twenty years, a quite remarkable series of finds have been made, some of them preserved as parks for the public. In fact, since the identification of these sites is almost always derived from detailed literary records of the period, the spots are not so much discovered as allowed to re-emerge.

The outer city wall of Song times was an irregular rectangle, wider at the north than the south. Walls stretched along the river on the east (the line of the rail line today), inland from the banks of the Qiantang River, and against West Lake on that side. The brick-faced walls are reported to be 30 Song feet (7 m) in height with a base of similar dimension and a width at the top of 10 Song feet (2.3 m). A total of thirteen gates breached this wall, with five water gates for boat traffic. The Imperial Way, over 13 km long and following the present Zhongshan Road, served as the city's axis, but the imperial city and palace were at the south, a placement that reversed canonical city plans (see Chs. 17 and 23). This position was forced on the court by natural topography. Thus only when proceeding to the altars in the hills southwest of the city did the emperor move south from his palace as custom expected. Many channels crossed the city (Polo compared Hangzhou, not Suzhou, to Venice), and roadways generally ran parallel to them. Merchants and other establishments could be approached either from the front by the street or from the rear by water. The 1.2 million residents were aug-

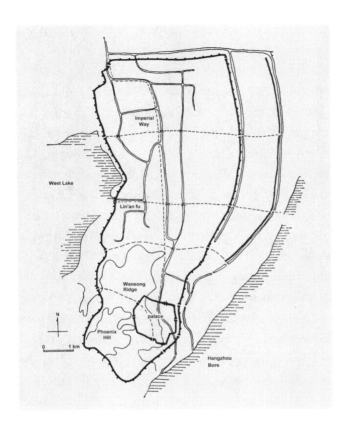

Plan of Southern Song Lin'an

mented by a large floating population who came to the city on business at its several hundred markets. The city was densely populated across all of its sixty-eight wards, unlike Chang'an or Dadu which never filled in, with many two-story buildings that visitors noted. More than fifty Buddhist temples and twenty Daoist ones occupied space within the city's walls.

The Song imperial city lies on low hills east of Phoenix Hill. Its walls are constructed of pounded earth and rubble with layers of dressed stone at the base and brick on the surface. They vary from 9 to 14 m thick and are visible in some areas. The north wall can be traced for over 700 m, running along the south of Wansongling Road uphill westward; the east wall runs down the west side of Mantoushan Road. The imperial palace, although modeled after the Northern Song Eastern Capital at Kaifeng, was essentially a single ensemble of halls rather than the expected series of courtyards. In fact, the name placard of the main hall—the only venue deemed suitable—was changed as different ceremonial needs and functions required. The site was purposefully destroyed by the Mongols in 1276 and lies deeply buried. Parts of the palace walls and several of its gates have been located. The Hening Gate, the rear (north) gate, actually served for most imperial purposes; the Imperial Way began from it. This thoroughfare north of the palace served as a de facto "outer court" with important ministries on both sides amid ordinary residences. The largest court assemblies, such as New Years, were held here, north of the palace.

Several imperial sites have been uncovered in the last ten years. The Imperial Ancestral Temple (Tai Miao) on the east slope of Ziyang Shan (Zhongshan South Road) is now a park. Built in 1134 and expanded several times, it stood amid the ministries flanking the Imperial Way. In principle, the Song emperors came here five times each year to offer sacrifices to their ancestors. The residence of the Gongsheng Renlie empress at the foot of Wushan was the target of a salvage excavation in 2001. Features preserved include the paving and foundations for two halls, a court yard, and galleries. The yard incorporated a large pond (12 by 7 m) with an artificial mountain of Lake Tai rock. The local government, the yamen of Lin'an, displaced from the old palace when the Song court arrived, was relocated near the Qingbo Gate of the city's west wall in 1165–73. In fact local administration remained here until the early twentieth century. The Song levels of this site at Hehuachitou were exposed in 2000; the complex is still partially occupied by contemporary buildings, but the excavated tracts reveal the same building materiel found at the Tai Miao and Empress' residence. Finally, the Deshou Palace, used as the retirement residence for the first two Southern Song emperors, Gaozong and Xiaozong, has been located near Wangxian Bridge between Wangjiang Road and Jixiang Lane.

Celadon

Among the famous products and resources of the Lower Yangzi macroregion—such as silks, tea, and hardwood furniture—are green-glazed ceramics known in English as "celadon." These high-fired ceramics date from the Bronze Age, when stonewares from the Yangzi drainage appear at Shang and Zhou sites across the north. The superior clays available in several regions, including Hangzhou, made this area a center for green wares from early times through the late imperial era. Important sites outside the Southern Song city at Wugui Shan and Laohudong document imperial kilns in the twelfth century that supported the needs of the court, especially for ritual objects.

The kiln near the Suburban Altar (Jiaotan) at Wugui Shan, about 2 km southwest of the Song imperial city, was rediscovered in the early twentieth century; preliminary work was conducted in the 1950s. It was not until 1985–86, however, that full-fledged excavations took place, exposing a "dragon kiln," several workshops, and 30,000 shards of celadon wasters. This site flourished from the early Southern Song, but seems not to have continued production under the Mongols. The second site, Laohudong, only 100m from the imperial city, was exposed after heavy rains in fall, 1996. This even larger complex had three dragon

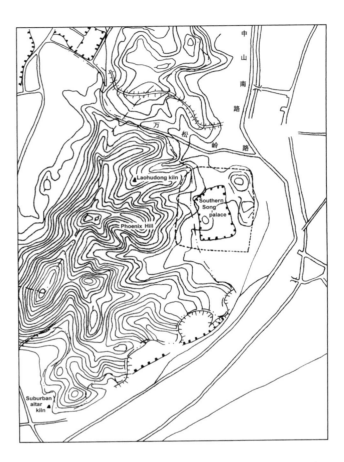

中山南路

万松岭路

Laohudong kiln

Southern Song palace

Phoenix Hill

Suburban altar kiln

Location of imperial kilns

kilns, four smaller "bun-shaped" kilns, and ten work-shops with requisite facilities: tanks for levigating clays, pivots for throwing wheels, and crocks for glaze. This site probably started before Southern Song and continued into the Yuan period.

Both kilns were in an area of the city that had become cemetery tracts. These graves have now been removed, and the site at Wugui Shan has been developed as the Southern Song Imperial Kiln Museum (Nan Song Guanyao Bowuguan), with displays tracing the history of green wares as well as the well-preserved dragon kiln.

Marco Polo's lengthy description of Hangzhou will be found in Ronald Latham, *Marco Polo: The Travels* (1958), pp. 213–31. Jacques Gernet, *Daily Life in China on the Eve of the Mongol Invasion, 1250–1276* (1962), esp. "The City," pp. 22–58, considers life at the time relying on Chinese sources. A scholarly treatment of Polo's account is A.C. Moule, *Quinsai with Other Notes on Marco Polo* (1957), pp. 1–53. On ceramics, consult Rosemary Scott, *Imperial Taste: Chinese Ceramics from the Percival David Foundation* (1989).

Guan yao *vase,
Laohudong*

23 Dadu: Khubilai Khan's City

BEIJING
YUAN PERIOD, 1260s–1368

China's capital first entered the European imagination as the "Khan's Great City" described by Marco Polo (1254–1324), a city known to its Chinese residents as Dadu (Great Capital). Dadu was a city designed and constructed afresh, one of the few Chinese capitals created from scratch (like Ch. 17, Sui-Tang Chang'an). Although in Beijing today little of the Yuan city can be seen or touched, the presence of Dadu is nonetheless strong. The Yuan capital determined the placement, size, and shape of the Ming-Qing city, the foundations of modern Beijing. The contemporary road grid and many features of the Imperial City and Forbidden City are its legacy.

Because the site of Dadu has been occupied continuously since the fifteenth century, the archaeology of the Yuan capital is often frustrating. Many discoveries have been fortuitous, byproducts of work on or repairs to infrastructure. For example, a Yuan-period marble bridge was uncovered north of the Xidan intersection; it was 38 m long with a water channel lined with stone below. South of Xisi, open drainage ditches along the sides of major Yuan roadways have also been found. In one of them a mason left an inscription dated 1328. A number of caches (porcelains, mirrors) have been found in and around the Yuan city. In the 1960s to 70s,

White Dagoba, Miaoying Si

pulling down the brick-faced Ming walls exposed the original earthen walls of Dadu on the east and west sides of the city. Water channels were found underneath and footings for the Yuan period corner towers and gates were also identified. On the west side, parts of the Heyi Gate were intact within the fabric of the Ming Xizhi Men. The demise of the Ming north wall was even more productive. It had been built in 1368 when the Ming commander Xu Da decided to make the city smaller. As a result, his new north wall rolled over Yuan-era *hutong* and residential structures along its path. Dozens of small finds and several large compounds were exposed when the Ming overburden was removed. The line of the Ming north wall corresponds to the south margin of the Second Ring Road. As Beijing prepares for the 2008 Olympic Games, still more traces of the Khan's city will surely come to light.

Cambaluc

When Genghis Khan began his conquest of North China, the Jin capital, Zhongdu, became his target. The city fell in 1215, and suffered serious destruction as punishment for the stiff resistance of its inhabitants. Genghis was soon involved elsewhere, and North China was parceled out to Mongol princes as appanages (fiefs). One of these was Genghis's grandson, Khubilai (1215–94), who in 1260 became the fifth Great Khan. Khubilai, while not literate in Chinese, acquired a coterie of Chinese advisors during his days in North China. These learned scholars had decisively affected the choice and design of a new capital in modern-day Inner Mongolia, called Shangdu (Coleridge's "Xanadu"). Chief among them was Liu Bingzhong (1216–74), a Confucian scholar and Buddhist. In 1260, Khubilai encamped north of the ruined Zhongdu on Qionghua Island in a lake within a former Jin palace. Khubilai and his advisors decided to create a new capital using the lake as the centerpiece of its imperial precincts. Work began in 1267.

Many names have been associated with the construction of Dadu. Liu and several other Chinese officials were advisors who "assisted the Khan" in devising the overall plan. This was derived from the "royal city" (*wang cheng*) described in the *Artificer's Record* (*Kaogongji*), an ancient text that specified essential traits for the capital of the Son of Heaven. Making the Mongol capital conform to this idealized model was part of a broad effort to establish the legitimacy of the conquest regime. Below these scholar advisors were supervisors who shouldered the actual burden of assembling men and materiel for the vast project. These included Yegdir (of Arab ancestry?), who headed the "tent service" responsible for yurts and other palace furnishings. He also served as Supervisor-in-Chief of All Classes of Artisans, the corps of skilled carpenters, masons, and brick makers who made building materials. Other Chinese participants included Zhang Honglue, who served as Supervisor for Building the Palace Enceinte, and Duan Tianyou, who headed the Branch Ministry of Works. The Grand Capital Garrison was also impressed into service, since much unskilled labor and many artisan families were drawn from the military. As with the Liao and Jin regimes before them, the Mongols depended on Han-Chinese craftsmen and laborers. By 1274, the new palace was completed; by 1284, the city's outer walls had been put up.

The Great Capital grew up around the shores of the lake that is the predecessor of the modern Bei Hai. In making this area the core of their new city, the planners relied on the Gaoliang River, a water source that enters the city from the west at the present-day Zizhu Park. The Chinese scholar Guo Shoujing is credited with suggesting that this river's supply be enhanced by tapping the Yuquan Shan spring in the present Summer Palace. The imperial lake came to be known as Taiye Chi and its island as Wansui Shan (Longevity Mountain). The latter was flanked on the south by a new, smaller man-made island, both connected to the shore by bridges. The Yuan imperial palaces flanked this idyllic setting: the Danei (Great Within) of the emperor to the east, and palaces for the Heir and Empress Dowager on the west. This ensemble of palaces and parks, the Imperial City, was demarcated by a modest red wall. This wall had a base only 3m wide, while the actual palace walls were 16 m wide!

The Khan's palace dictated the central axis of the city as a whole, but unlike the classical "royal city" plan, it was not located at the center. Instead the palace was shifted south, and designed as a rectangle about 1000 m north–south by 740 m east–west (almost the same dimensions as the Ming Forbidden City). The Danei was divided in turn into a front, Daming Palace, and a rear, Yanchun Pavilion. The former had a three-tiered platform supporting its front hall, with an elevated corridor leading to the rear hall. (This platform is echoed by the Ming "Three Great Halls of State.") Gates, bell and drum towers, and another rear hall were embedded in the perimeter galleries. A wide avenue separated this palace from the rear ensemble, which centered on a two-story pavilion in an even larger rectangular yard. Other compounds including storehouses and kitchens flanked these two main yards.

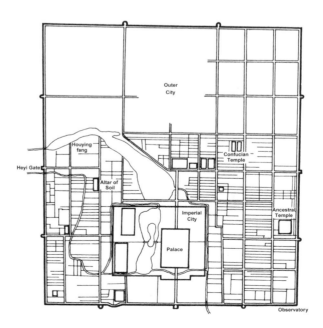

Plan: Dadu

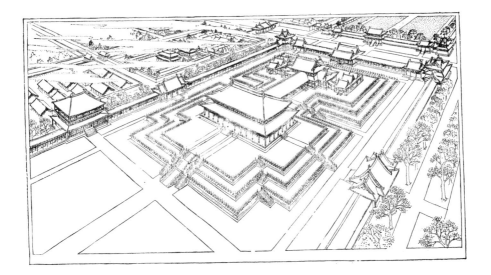

Behind the rear compound was an imperial park where tents apparently were often pitched, a nod to Mongol preferences. The Yuan palace lies under the present-day Forbidden City and Jingshan Park. The palace south gate was at about the position of the present Taihe Dian (Hall of Supreme Harmony), while the rear gate was on the north side of Jingshan. The Yuan capital's axis, running through the main halls, later became the axis of the Ming-Qing city, running from the Bell and Drum Towers south through the Forbidden City to the Front Gate.

Eventually palaces for the heir and empress dowager were built west of the lake and islands. The compound on the south designed for the Heir was the Longfu Gong. The palace on the north for the Empress Dowager, the Xingsheng Gong, had its own walled compound equal in size to the Yanchun Pavilion as well as a park at rear. The areas occupied by these palaces correspond to parts of today's Zhongnan Hai, home of the PRC leadership, and Bei Hai Park.

Rendering by Fu Xinian of Yuan palace halls

The position of the Dadu city walls derived from surveys made from a point north of the palace, the Central Stele Pavilion (Zhongxin Zhi Tai). Equal distances east, south, west, and north from this point determined the alignment of the walls. The distance available on the south was constrained by the ruins of Zhongdu, the old Jin capital, still inhabited and partially walled. Although the four measurements are in fact roughly equal, the east wall was pulled slightly west to avoid marshy ground. The east-west and north-south dimensions for the city may have been conceived as multiples of those for the Danei. Fu Xinian has pointed out that the Yuan city was nine Danei-widths wide (east-west) and five Danei-lengths long (north-south). Likewise, the area of the Ming Forbidden City served as a module for the area of the Ming city, as Fu has demonstrated. The outer walls of Dadu measured 28.6 km in circumference when the Institute of Archaeology performed a modern survey in the 1960s and 70s. The south wall ran along the south side of Chang'an Boulevard, while the east and west walls were identical with those of the Ming city (and hence today's Second Ring Road). The north wall of Dadu still survives as the Earthen Wall (Tu Cheng, now strip parks) about half way between the Third and Fourth Ring Roads.

The Yuan city wall utilized earthen construction, the pounded earth technique. During the modern survey, the base was found to average 24 m across; lengths varied from 6690 m (the south wall) to 7600 m (west wall). Earth needed for this task was dug from the outside of the wall, creating a moat in the process. Water for the moat was drawn from the Gaoliang River, and generally flowed by gravity from the west to the southeast, where the moats joined the Tonghui Canal. Intact portions of the Yuan wall suggest an original height of about 16 m, top width about 8 m. (This is higher than the wall around the Forbidden City or the Ming Inner City wall flanking the Front Gate.) Made of a combination of loess soil, lime, and broken shards of tile and brick with imbedded wooden stakes, the wall was very sturdy, but nonetheless susceptible to weather. To protect its top, tiles were laid to draw off water, and reed matting was used to cover the sides. The four corners of the city had watch towers, whose bases were identified during the 1960s survey. One of these towers actually survives in the foundations of the Ming Imperial Observatory (Guan Xiang Tai) near Jianguo Men.

Eleven gates (not twelve as Polo writes) controlled access to the city, three each on the east, south, and west, and two on the north. These points were fortified with guard houses over timber-frame portals. Wooden bridges crossed the moats. Later, these gates were improved by the construction of barbican gates, a semi-circular wall and second portal directly in front of the main gate. One of these barbican gates was uncovered in the process of tearing down Xizhi Men in 1969. It stood 22 m tall, with a passage 9 m long and over 4 m wide. Atop the portal was the paving for a three-room guard house; stairs permitted the guards to ascend. An artisan's inscription of 1358 confirmed its construction date. The gate and portal was remade in the Ming as a brick, barrel vault structure and served Xizhi Men thereafter.

The Yuan city gates determined the position of the main arteries of the capital grid. The two northern gates in the east and west walls and the two gates of the north wall were all abandoned when the city contracted after the Ming victory in 1368. The other four gates of the east and west walls, however, continued in use through Ming, Qing, and modern times, albeit with changes in names. As the Ming capital was built in the early fifteenth century for the Yongle Emperor, the original Yuan south wall was torn down. Its three gates were re-established at new positions further south, now Second Ring Road. The main arteries of Dadu crisscrossed the city creating a regular grid, but only two extended unimpeded from one wall to its opposite. These primary arteries were about 37 m wide; secondary roads were half that width (18 m), and the ubiquitous alleys (*hutong*) half of that (9 m). (*Hutong* is loosely applied to many alleys; it comes from a Mongol term, *hottog*, meaning "water well.") Areas within major arteries were designated as residential wards, for a total of fifty. Unlike the wards of Tang Chang'an, these were not walled and gated. Probing in the 1960s outside the Ming north wall revealed twenty-two parallel alleys between adjacent gates. The distance between these alleys was 77 m, ample space for a house three courtyards deep. Large government establishments were built on rectangular plots measuring multiple *hutong* long and wide. The Ancestral Temple and Altar of Soil, for example, each were assigned plots of five by four *hutong*; lesser establishments were in plots four by three *hutong*. Most of the alleys in today's city north of Chang'an Boulevard are in fact those laid out when Dadu was surveyed.

Circulation within Dadu cannot have been easy. All the primary and secondary arteries in the south half of the city were interrupted by the Imperial City and the lakes that stored water north of it. On the other hand,

by the 1290s the Tonghui Canal connected the city to
the distant southeast. Boats and barges carrying all
manner of goods sailed directly into the city, north
along the east side of the Imperial City (Heyan Street),
and on to a great market west of the Central Stele
Pavilion (today's Hou Hai). Other markets grew on
both the east and west sides of the city near modern
Xisi and Dengshikou, as well as around the three gates
of the south wall. Unlike alien regimes before them, the
Mongols did not segregate people by ethnic groups. A
diverse international population lived throughout the
city. Likewise, unlike Tang Chang'an and other capitals,
the main organs of state were dispersed around the city,
as were state depots and temples.

Only a few features from the Khan's capital can still be
experienced. Bei Hai Park offers views of the city

Yuan Heyi Gate
(Xizhi Men)

Yuan Remains

Courtyard house under
Ming wall
(Houyingfang)

from its White Dagoba (Qing period), which sits atop the hill that in Khubilai's day was the highest point in the city. Much enhanced and expanded toward the south, the three lakes are descendants of the Taiye Chi of the Yuan Imperial City. The White Dagoba (Bai Ta) of Miaoying Si is the only substantial monument of Yuan date (1271–79) in the city itself. Its precincts are much reduced, and its buildings, with the notable exception of the dagoba itself, are all Qing-era structures. The Confucian Temple (1302–06), also an ensemble of Qing buildings, has both a plan and ancient cypress trees that date to the Yuan. Finally, well north of the city on the way to the Great Wall at Badaling is the "Cloud Terrace" (Yuntai) at Juyong Guan, the base of a pagoda erected in the late Yuan (1345) over the main route from Shangdu to Dadu. This is the outstanding work of the Yuan period in Beijing, and well worth a special stop for its impressive reliefs and multi-lingual inscriptions.

Another archaeological site preserved in the city is the Water Gate from the south wall of Zhongdu, the Jin capital. The Liao Jin City Wall Museum is located south of You'an Men outside of the Outer City moat (the Third Ring Road). Good displays that illustrate the history of the city are also found at the Capital Museum within the Confucian Temple and at Bai Ta.

Morris Rossabi has written a readable biography of *Khubilai Khan: His Life and Times* (1988). Marco Polo describes Dadu (which he called Cambaluc) in passages that may reflect a mixture of firsthand encounters and hearsay about the "Great Within." See *Marco Polo: the Travels* (1958), pp. 124–31. Frances Wood's *Did Marco Polo Go to China?* (1996) is a stimulating, but too often uncritical, negative answer to the perennial question.

Cloud Terrace, Juyong Guan

24 Dingling: The Ming Valley

DINGLING MUSEUM
CHANGPING, BEIJING
MING PERIOD, 1409–1620
WORLD HERITAGE SITE

In 1955, the vice mayor of Beijing proposed opening the Changling, tomb of Zhu Di, better known as the Yongle emperor (r. 1403–24), the man who built Beijing. The State Council quickly gave its approval and a working group was then established. According to later accounts, this group decided to excavate a less challenging tomb first as preparation for the main event. So it was that work began instead on the Dingling—the tomb of the Zhu Xiangjun, the Wanli emperor (d. 1620)—in June of 1956. Opening this tomb proved moderately difficult, but clearing its chambers and conserving objects was even more so. Two years later, the advocates of excavating the Changling decided not to proceed. Reading between the lines, it appears there was in fact considerable opposition from the outset to excavating any of the Ming imperial tombs. China was not prepared, said these critics, to take responsibility for what archaeologists might find. The resulting losses would be irretrievable. Indeed, the sad condition of the imperial robes and silk textiles taken out of the Dingling supports the reservations of Xia Nai and other opponents at the time.

Stone general along
Spirit Path, Ming valley

Like all imperial capitals, Beijing required imperial tombs. Yongle's advisors selected a pleasant valley 40 km north of the capital in the foothills of the Tianshou Mountains. This was actually the fourth location designated for imperial burials. The Ming founder, Zhu Yuanzhang (Hongwu, r. 1368–98), had sited his tomb, the Xiaoling, east of Nanjing. He also established a burial for his grandfather in Sihong, Jiangsu, and tombs for his parents in Fengyang, Anhui. Following these models, but especially the Xiaoling, Yongle began work on his own tomb in 1409, and as it happened interred his empress, née Xu, soon thereafter. As the first emperor to utilize the site, Yongle chose a location near the center of the valley nestled against the eastern hills. Over the next two hundred years, twelve more Ming emperors were buried here. None of their tombs, however, match the scale of Changling. (The last Ming emperor, a suicide, was buried ignominiously in a tomb already prepared for one of his consorts.)

After some depredations upon the fall of the dynasty in 1644, especially at the Dingling, the Manchu court protected the valley. The Qing even restored some tombs, including the sacrificial hall at the Dingling. Today, however, most of the above-ground structures in the valley are in ruinous condition; only at Changling does the original sacrificial hall survive. The valley of the "Thirteen Tombs of the Ming" (Ming Shisan Ling) was placed on the national register in 1961. With the advent of extensive tourism, the valley has become one of the most visited locales in the Beijing region. With the two clusters of Qing imperial tombs, the Ming valley is now enrolled as a World Heritage Site.

The Thirteen Ming Tombs: Spirit Path

On the way into the Ming valley, one first encounters a massive marble ceremonial archway built in 1540 and now on the east side of the road. This structure mimics the timber arches that once punctuated all major crossroads of the capital, albeit here on a massive scale and with five bays. The archway marks the approach to the imperial tombs, a tradition documented from the Han period.

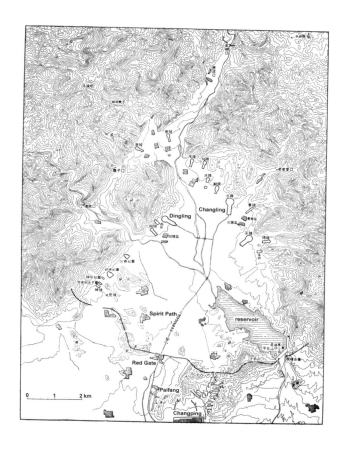

Map of the Ming valley

A red brick wall once encircled the 40 sq km of the valley floor and surrounding hills, manned by a garrison from nearby Changping. Its main entrance, the Great Red Gate, resembles the Great Ming Gate that led to the Imperial City of the capital. The gate has a yellow-tile roof over solid red masonry and three portals. Behind this gate stands a huge stele pavilion, also red with yellow tile, housing a stone slab almost 8 m in height that proclaims the tomb of Yongle. The text was written by the emperor's son and erected in 1435 by his grandson. Four marble pillars flank Yongle's stele pavilion, comparable to those that attend

Detail of ceremonial arch

the Gate of Heavenly Peace in Beijing. Thus the entrance of the valley makes an explicit equation between itself and the Imperial City, as residences of the Son of Heaven in life and in death. (Compare remarks on the Tang imperial tombs, Ch. 18.)

The ceremonial approach, the "Spirit Path" built for Yongle's own tomb, actually came to serve all thirteen sites. While the oldest prototypes for such a path are found at Nanjing with tombs of the Southern Dynasties (Ch. 14), the custom has even more ancient roots. Now free from traffic, the Spirit Path is a restful area shaded in season by luxuriant willows. The sequence of stone carvings flanking the path starts with a pair of pillars, and continues over the next 1060m with twenty-four pairs of stone animals in standing and kneeling postures and twelve pairs of officials. The selection of animals and figures is indebted to the Tang and Song imperial tombs, the two native dynasties the Ming emulated. Yet another stone ceremonial gateway marks the end of this pathway; its design can be found at the Temple of Heaven in Beijing. Crossing a stone bridge farther into the valley, the first left turn leads to the Dingling.

The Wanli emperor, Zhu Xiangjun, built his tomb over a period of six years beginning in 1584. He visited the site several times during his reign, and lived for thirty years after its completion. A conservative estimate suggests the cost of the tomb over that period was equivalent to the total revenue of the imperial court for two years. It served as a resting place both for the emperor and two consorts.

Dingling

Like all of the Ming tombs, the Dingling is a walled precinct, rectangular in overall plan but with a rounded north wall. The front portions of this precinct are a series of broad courtyards divided by gates and walls. The approach leads through two outer gates to the gate of the Offering Hall (Ling'en Dian) to the hall itself. Although this architectural setting is akin to the Forbidden City, the ancient trees and plantings here set this world apart from the more severe palace yards. At Dingling, only the stone platforms of the gate and main hall, with balustrades and ramps, survive. (After restoration by the Qing, they later burned.) Behind the sacrificial hall foundation is a stone altar table with stone fittings—a tripod incense burner, two vases, and two candle sticks. This complement of accessories is found at all imperial sites, such the Temple of Heaven. The altar is situated under the open sky before the burial mound. Faced with the same gray brick used in the walls of Beijing and the Forbidden City, this mound is fronted by a masonry tower that holds a stele commemorating Wanli. The view of the valley from the parapet is well worth the climb. The entrance to the underground burial chambers lies beyond.

Excavation of Dingling

In 1956 no other imperial tomb had been properly excavated in China, and no one could be certain what might lie within. The excavators enjoyed remarkable luck. They first noticed that some bricks in the wall surrounding the mound west of the main axis had subsided. Opening a trench against the wall, they found themselves on a stone and brick ramp helpfully labeled as such by inscription (*sui dao men,* roughly "the gate to the entrance ramp"). This access ramp wound east back toward the central axis. To save time, and to avoid disturbing the ancient pine trees growing on the mound, the team opened another trench on axis midway between the stele tower and the crown of the

Plan of Dingling chambers

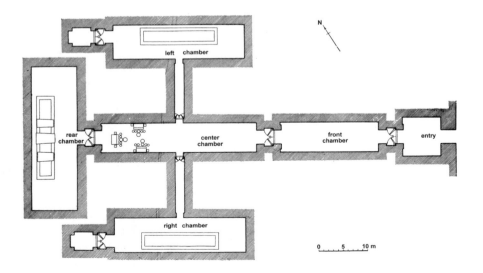

mound. Here their good fortune continued: a stone left by the builders also had an inscription—"160 feet at a depth of 35 feet"—detailing the distance to the outer wall of the burial chambers. Finally, by opening a third trench near the center of the mound, the excavators reached the bricked-up opening to the chambers. (Between the tower and the chamber yet another slab carrying an inscription later came to light, this one describing the position of the chamber's front wall.) The explicit directions rediscovered by archaeologists had been left by the tomb's builders, knowing their need to re-open the chambers for later interments. Gaining entry, however, posed one last challenge. A self-locking door barred access. The locking mechanism was a slab that had fallen into place after the panels were closed from the outside, anchored by slots in the doors and floor. (Similar contrivances were found in the Nan Yue, Ch. 11, and Mancheng Han tombs.) An ingenious worker used a wire inserted between the door panels to yank the slab out of position.

The burial that awaited the excavators was of gigantic scale: the front chamber a vaulted space 20 m long and 6 m wide with an interior height of 7.2 m; the central chamber even longer at 32 m, with similar width and height; and across the axis a rear chamber 30 m long and 9 m wide. The chambers on axis were flanked by two parallel rooms of similar scale. All five chambers were stone, barrel vault construction, highly polished marble that showed not a trace of deterioration. Large ceramic tiles were used for flooring, the same kind that glistens in the palace halls of the Forbidden City.

Today the chambers are largely empty. At the time they were opened, however, decayed timbers were found covering the floor from front door to the rear, probably to protect the surface as the huge coffins were installed. Three stone thrones were arrayed at the rear of the central chamber, each accompanied by a small altar set like that above ground and large blue-and-white porcelain crocks that held oil for lamps. In the rear chamber were three large wooden double coffins on a low platform. All had decayed and collapsed, but their contents had never been disturbed. (The side chambers were not used during the two consort funerals.) Within these coffins and the chests placed at either side, the excavators retrieved large quantities of imperial robes and other textiles, plus many gold, silver, and jade objects (2600 items by official count). Many of these valuables are now displayed at the Changling, within its imposing sacrificial hall. A visit should conclude with the latter site.

The Tradition of Imperial Tombs

For anyone interested in archaeology, imperial tomb sites are an important part of a visit to China. Many common threads can be traced from the first imperial necropolis (Ch. 9, Lishan) through the Han, Tang, and Song periods. Prime real estate outside the capital, preferably high ground with good geomantic features, a processional path adorned with monumental stone carvings, a man-made mound or even natural mountain, and brick or stone underground chambers are common denominators.

The Ming plan, however, utilized a well-defined precinct sharing a common entrance and processional path. This contrasts with the immense landscape devoted to the Han and Tang imperial tombs near Xi'an (eleven and eighteen separate sites, respectively), and the nine clusters of burials for the Northern Song emperors in Henan. Although there are some exceptions, the Ming emperors were usually accompanied by their principal consorts, from one to three, in the same chamber. Lesser-ranking women and other court figures were excluded from the valley; there are no satellite burials. Most Ming consorts were buried in Haidian District of suburban Beijing. In plan, the integration of front courtyards and rear mounds within a single wall also sets the Ming tombs apart from their predecessors. The Qing tombs followed Ming customs, both at their pre-conquest capital, Shenyang, and in the Eastern and Western tombs outside Beijing.

Being enfoeffed at important regional centers dispersed across the map, the Ming princes built their own tombs near their fiefs. Notable Ming princely tombs have been reported in Shandong, Henan, Shaanxi, Shanxi, Hubei, Hunan, Jiangxi, Sichuan, and Guangxi. These tombs are often rich repositories of valuable ceramics and jewelry of the deceased.

SUGGESTED READING

A fascinating account of the Wanli emperor's era is Ray Huang's *1587, A Year of No Significance: The Ming Dynasty in Decline* (1981). *The Imperial Ming Tombs* by Ann Paludan (1981) is a useful guide to the valley with many drawings and photographs. For the larger context, see Susan Naquin, *Peking: Temples and City Life, 1400–1900* (2000).

Bibliography

Bagley, Robert, ed. *Ancient Sichuan: Treasures from a Lost Civilization* (Seattle: Seattle Art Museum, 2001).

Barber, Elizabeth Wayland. *The Mummies of Urumchi* (New York: Norton, 1999).

Benewick, Robert and Stephanie Donald. *The State of China Atlas* (Harmondsworth: Penguin, 2005).

Birrell, Anne. *Chinese Mythology* (Baltimore: Johns Hopkins University Press, 1993).

_____, *The Classic of Mountains and Seas* (Harmondsworth: Penguin, 1999).

Blunden, Caroline and Mark Elvin. *A Cultural Atlas of China* (New York: Facts on File, 1983).

Boaz, Noel T. and Russell L. Ciochon. *Dragon Bone Hill: An Ice-Age Saga of Homo Erectus* (Oxford: Oxford University Press, 2004).

Bower, Virginia L. *From Court to Caravan: Tomb Sculpture from the Collection of Anthony M. Solomon* (Cambridge: Harvard University Art Museums, 2002).

Chang, Kwang-chih. *The Archaeology of Ancient China,* 4th ed. (New Haven: Yale University Press, 1986).

Chang, Kwang-chih and Xu Pingfang, et al. *The Formation of Chinese Civilization: An Archaeological Perspective,* ed. Sarah Allan. The Culture and Civilization of China (New Haven: Yale University Press, 2005).

Cook, Constance and John Major, eds. *Defining Chu: Image and Reality in Ancient China* (Honolulu: University of Hawaii Press, 1999).

Creel, Herrlee G. *The Origins of Statecraft in China: The Western Chou Empire* (Chicago: University of Chicago Press, 1970).

Debaine-Francfort, Corinne. *The Search for Ancient China* (New York: Harry N. Abrams, 1999).

Falkenhausen, Lothar von. *Suspended Music: Chime-Bells in the Culture of Bronze Age China* (Berkeley: University of California Press, 1993).

Fong, Wen, ed. *The Great Bronze Age of China* (New York: Metropolitan Museum of Art, 1980).

Fu Xinian et al. *Chinese Architecture,* ed. N. Steinhardt. The Culture and Civilization of China (New Haven: Yale University Press, 2002).

Gernet, Jacques. *Buddhism in Chinese Society: An Economic and Social History from the Fifth to the Tenth Centuries* (New York: Columbia University Press, 1995).

_____. *Daily Life in China on the Eve of the Mongol Invasion 1250–1276* (New York: Macmillan, 1962).

_____. *A History of Chinese Civilization* (Cambridge: Cambridge University Press, 1982).

Han Yu, "Memorial on the Bone of the Buddha," in W. T. de Bary and I. Bloom, eds., *Sources of Chinese Tradition,* 2nd ed. (New York: Columbia University Press, 1999), vol. 1, pp. 583–85.

Hawkes, David. *The Songs of the South* (Harmondsworth: Penguin, 1985).

Henricks, Robert G., trans. *Lao Tzu: Te-Tao ching* (New York: Ballantine, 1989).

Hopkirk, Peter. *Foreign Devils on the Silk Road* (Amherst: University of Massachusetts Press, 1980).

Huang, Ray. *1587: A Year of No Significance* (New Haven: Yale University Press, 1981).

Hulsewé, A.F.P. *China in Central Asia, the Early Stage: 125 B.C.–23 A.D.* (Leiden: Brill, 1979).

Jia Lanpo and Huang Weiwen. *The Story of Peking Man: From Archaeology to Mystery* (Hong Kong: Oxford University Press, 1990).

Juliano, Annette L. and Judith A. Lerner, eds. *Monks and Merchants: Silk Road Treasures from Northwest China, Gansu, and Ningxia Provinces, 4th–7th Centuries* (New York: Asia Society, 2001).

Ledderose, Lothar. *Ten Thousand Things: Module and Mass Production in Chinese Art* (Princeton: Princeton University Press, 2000).

Li Chi. *Anyang* (Seattle: University of Washington Press, 1977).

Li Xueqin, trans. K.C. Chang. *Eastern Zhou and Qin Civilizations* (New Haven: Yale University Press, 1985).

Liang Ssu-ch'eng. *A Pictorial History of Chinese Architecture: A Study of the Development of Its Structural System and the Evolution of Its Types,* ed. Wilma Fairbank (Cambridge, Mass: MIT Press, 1984).

Liu Li. *The Chinese Neolithic: Trajectories to Early States* (Cambridge: Cambridge University Press, 2004).

Loewe, M. and E.L. Shaughnessy, eds. *The Cambridge History of Ancient China: From the Origins of Civilization to 221 B.C.* (Cambridge: Cambridge University Press, 1999).

Major, John and Jenny F. So, eds. *Music in the Age of Confucius* (Washington, D.C.: Sackler Gallery, 2000).

Mallory, J.P. and Victor H. Mair. *The Tarim Mummies: Ancient China and the Mystery of the Earliest Peoples from the West* (London: Thames and Hudson, 2000).

Mirsky, Jeannette. *Sir Mark Aurel Stein: Archaeological Explorer* (Chicago: University of Chicago, 1977).

Mote, Frederick W. *Imperial China: 900–1800* (Harvard University Press, 1999).

Moule, A.C. *Quinsai with Other Notes on Marco Polo* (Cambridge: University Press, 1957).

Naquin, Susan. *Peking: Temples and City Life, 1400–1900* (Berkeley: University of California Press, 2000).

Nickel, Lukas, ed. *Return of the Buddha: the Qingzhou Discoveries* (London: Royal Academy of Arts, 2002).

Paludan, Ann. *The Imperial Ming Tombs* (New Haven: Yale University Press, 1981).

_____, *The Chinese Spirit Road: The Classical Tradition of Stone Tomb Statuary* (New Haven: Yale University Press, 1991).

Marco Polo: The Travels, trans. and ed. Ronald Latham, (Harmondsworth: Penguin, 1958).

The Quest for Eternity (Los Angeles: Los Angeles County Museum of Art, 1987).

Rossabi, Morris. *Khubilai Khan: His Life and Times* (Berkeley: University of California Press, 1988).

Schafer, Edward. *The Golden Peaches of Samarkand: A Study of T'ang Exotics* (Berkeley: University of California Press, 1963).

Scott, Rosemary. *Imperial Taste: Chinese Ceramics from the Percival David Foundation* (Los Angeles: Los Angeles County Museum of Art, 1989).

Shapiro, Harry. *Peking Man: The Discovery, Disappearance and Mystery of a Priceless Scientific Treasure* (New York: Simon and Schuster, 1974).

Shaughnessy, Edward L., trans. *I Ching: The Classic of Changes* (New York: Ballantine: 1996).

Spiro, Audrey. *Contemplating the Ancients: Aesthetic and Social Issues in Early Chinese Portraiture* (Berkeley, CA: University of California Press, 1990).

Steinhardt, Nancy Shatzman. *Liao Architecture* (Honolulu: University of Hawaii Press, 1997).

Thorp, Robert L. *China in the Early Bronze Age: Shang Civilization* (Philadelphia: University of Pennsylvania Press, 2005).

Thorp, Robert L. and Richard Ellis Vinograd. *Chinese Art and Culture* (New York: Abrams, 2001).

Tuan, Yi-fu. *China, The World's Landscapes* (Chicago: Aldine, 1969).

Twitchett, Denis, ed. *The Cambridge History of China*, vol. 3, *Sui-T'ang China, 589–906* (Cambridge: Cambridge University Press, 1979).

Twitchett, Denis and Michael Loewe, eds. *The Cambridge History of China*, vol. 1, *The Ch'in and Han Empires, 221 B.C.-A.D. 220* (Cambridge: Cambridge University Press, 1986).

Waley, Arthur, trans. *The Book of Songs* (1937).

_____. *Ballads and Stories from Tun-huang* (London: Allen and Unwin, 1960).

Wang Zhongshu, trans. K.C. Chang and Collaborators. *Han Civilization* (New Haven: Yale University Press, 1982).

Watson, Burton, trans. *Records of the Grand Historian*, 2 vols. (New York: Columbia University Press, 1961).

Watt, James C.Y., ed. *China: Dawn of a Golden Age, 200–750 A.D.* (New York: Metropolitan Museum of Art, 2004).

Wechsler, Howard. *Offerings of Jade and Silk: Ritual and Symbol in the Legitimation of the T'ang Dynasty* (New Haven: Yale University Press, 1985).

Whitfield, Roderick and Anne Farrer. *The Caves of the Thousand Buddhas* (London: British Museum, 1990).

Whitfield, Roderick, Susan Whitfield, and Neville Agnew. *Cave Temples of Mogao* (Los Angeles: Getty Conservation Institute, 2000).

Whitfield, Susan, ed. *The Silk Road: Trade, Travel, War and Faith* (Chicago: Serindia, 2004).

Wood, Frances. *Did Marco Polo Go to China?* (Boulder: Westview Press, 1995).

Xiong, Victor C. *Sui-Tang Chang'an: A Study in the Urban History of Medieval China* (Ann Arbor: Center for Chinese Studies, University of Michigan, 2000).

Yang, Xiaoneng, ed. *The Golden Age of Chinese Archaeology* (Washington, D.C.: National Gallery of Art, 1999).

_____, ed. *New Perspectives on China's Past: Chinese Archaeology in the Twentieth Century,* 2 vols. (New Haven: Yale University Press, 2004).

Yang Xuanzhi (Yang Hsuan-chih). *Record of the Buddhist Monasteries in Luoyang,* trans. Wang I-t'ung (Princeton: Princeton University Press, 1984).

_____. *Memories of Luoyang,* trans. W.J.F. Jenner (London: Oxford University Press, 1983).

Yates, Robin D.S., trans. *Five Lost Classics: Tao, Huang-Lao, and Yin-Yang in Han China* (New York: Ballantine, 1996).

Floating World Editions publishes books that contribute to a deeper understanding of Asian cultures. Editorial supervision: Ray Furse. Book and cover design: Liz Trovato. Production supervision: Bill Rose. Printing and binding: Malloy Incorporated. The typeface used is Bembo.